Jonathan,

Enjoy the incredible story of the Creation of the original Jeeps in images!

Blessings!

Paul Bruno 9/26/23

The Original Jeeps in Pictures

Jonathan,
I've ridden in a bunch of Jeeps of all ages — & they all still have the original's "bones"! Best Wishes
10/20/2023

by

Paul R. Bruno

First Edition

THE ORIGINAL JEEPS

IN PICTURES

FIRST EDITION

ISBN: 979-8-218-00911-3

Library of Congress Control Number: 2022939095

Design of Cover, Layout, Typography and Editing by M. Freedman

Published by MFM Publishing Division of Max Freedman Media, Los Angeles, California 90064, U.S.A.

Time Line—The Original Jeeps

1918–January 1940:	Project Genesis, research into a light vehicle
February–Mid-May 1940:	Discussions on light vehicle general characteristics
Mid-May–June 6, 1940:	Coalescing and documentation of vehicle general characteristics
June 6–June 20, 1940:	Initial work to develop a detailed vehicle specification
June 21–July 2, 1940:	Development and documentation of detailed vehicle drawing and specification
July 3–July 11, 1940:	Preparation and finalization of invitation for bids
July 12- July 21, 1940:	Bid preparation by manufacturers
July 22, 1940:	Bid opening and award to Bantam
July 22–July 24, 1940:	Willys given permission by QMC to build a pilot model at their own expense
July 23-August 5, 1940:	Finalization of bid award and contract award for Bantam
August 5-Sept. 21, 1940:	Bantam pilot model built and christened "Bantam Reconnaissance Car" (BRC)
August 15–November 4, 1940:	Willys pilot model built and named the Quad
September 23, 1940:	BRC delivered to Camp Holabird
Sept. 24-Oct. 23, 1940:	BRC tested at Camp Holabird
October 4, 1940:	Ford representatives, on invitation from the QMC, meet with QMC representatives who request they build and submit a pilot model
October 4–November 21, 1940:	Ford pilot model built and dubbed the Pygmy
October 4–December 3, 1940:	Order for 500 from each manufacturer becomes 1,500 from each contender
Oct. 23-29, 1940:	Inspection, test and final reports on Bantam pilot model completed
October 30, 1940:	BRC officially accepted and order for next sixty-nine placed

November 13, 1940	Willys Quad delivered to Camp Holabird
November 23, 1940	Ford Pygmy delivered to Camp Holabird
November 1940–January 1941:	Bantam builds the other 69 from original contract; Willys Quad and Ford Pygmy tested at Camp Holabird
January 6, 1941	Ford pilot model accepted and order for 1,500 vehicles commences
January 8–28, 1941:	Willys pilot model rejected and order for 1,500 cancelled
January 31–February 11, 1941:	Willys 1,500 unit order restored
February–June 1941:	Bantam and Ford build their 1,500
February 1941–May 1941:	Creation of the Willys MA
June 1941:	Willys MA goes into volume production
July 1941:	RFP for 16,000 vehicles
August 1941:	Award for 16,000 trucks to Willys-Overland Motors
August–October 1941:	Creation of the Willys MB
October–November 1941:	Formalization of agreement between, Willys, Ford and the QMC for Ford to build the MB under license

Dedication

To the late Cathy E. Bruno, Ph.D., my beloved wife, companion and soul mate who supported me, and the telling of this story.

I am incredibly indebted to my parents, the late Miriam and Victor Bruno, and my brothers, Eric and Karl Bruno, for always being there for me and all my other family and friends who sustained me during the journey.

Acknowledgements

There is no "I" in "team" states a popular phrase and though "I" wrote this book many individuals comprised the "team" that assisted in the journey.

I wish to thank Manuel "Max" Freedman, writing mentor and dear friend, for sharing his wisdom, and for editing and publishing the book. Steven Hoese, best friend, and research partner. Bill Mertens, another best friend, and research partner. Tatyana and Svetlana Senchihina of Two Organized for helping organize my research documents from 1941.

Linda Burkley, of Butler, PA for her support of telling this story over many years. Robert Brandon also of Butler, PA, for sharing the rare photographs of the building of the Bantam pilot model. JimBob Donze for supporting my books in Butler, PA and beyond.

Patrick R. Foster, author and automotive historian, for providing numerous photographs documenting Willys-Overland's history.

The Butler County Historical Society for providing photographs of downtown Butler circa 1940, the American Bantam Car Company factory and the Butler County Fairgrounds.

I am indebted to the archivists at the United States Archives, College Park, Maryland, who were always helpful and thoroughly professional as well as Bill Norris for sharing key documentation. Last but certainly not least, my nuclear family, the late Miriam and Victor Bruno, parents who helped me become who I am, and the best sister-in-laws and brothers anyone could ever have, Rebecca and Eric Bruno and Julie and Karl Bruno.

Finally, deep thanks to my late wife Cathy E. Bruno, Ph.D. It was her love, support and encouragement that made this book possible.

—Paul R. Bruno, Henderson, Nevada – 2022

Table of Contents

CHAPTER 1

The United States Army Between the Wars

1930 U.S. Army recruitment poster photograph. Source: U.S. Army Archives via Alamy Ltd.

British Troops in World War I

The United States Army, a victor in World War I, dramatically declined afterward. The "peace decade" of the 1920s, combined with a woeful domestic economy in the 1930s, played a significant role in the lack of readiness of the Army for war in 1940.

Source: Public Domain

George Washington

In 1796, under George Washington, the US instituted a policy of "no foreign entanglements". The US adhered to the president's guidance into the early 20th century. However, the policy severely limited military spending in the 1920s and 1930s, as well as diminished the United States' involvement in world affairs.

Source: Public Domain

Versailles Treaty

The treaty of Versailles officially ended World War I. However, the harsh provisions of the treaty imposed on the Germans were a major factor that helped lead to another world war in 1939.

Source: Public Domain

Calvin Coolidge

The 1920s witnessed severe limitations on United States Federal Government spending, including for the military. President Calvin "Silent Cal" Coolidge was the embodiment of this conservative budgeting philosophy.

Source: Public Domain

Calvin Coolidge Signs Kellogg-Briand Pact

The decade of the 1920s, known as the "peace decade"—so named due to a lack of military threats. Agreements such as the Kellogg-Briand pact signified a desire to avoid war. However, the absence of armed aggression would disappear in the 1930s.

Source: Library of Congress, Underwood & Underwood

The Great Depression

The Great Depression began in 1929, a catastrophe which saw economies collapse around the world. This led to the rise of dictatorships in Europe and Asia which increased militarism. For the United States, the Depression led to even further reductions in military spending.

Source: Public Domain

Reichstag Burning – 1933

Adolf Hitler became Chancellor of Germany in 1933. In February 1933 the Nazis used the destruction of the Reichstag to justify eliminating their opponents. With Hitler's rise to power, Germany began its march to war.

Source: Public Domain

The Rhineland – 1936

Hitler quickly rebuilt Geman military strength after assuming power. He began an aggressive campaign of conquest by annexing the Rhineland in violation of the Versailles Treaty. The West's lack of response emboldened the Nazi leader to risk further aggression.

Source: Public Domain

The Munich Agreement – 1938

Hitler annexed Austria in 1938. In an attempt to appease him the Western powers signed the Munich Agreement in the fall of 1938. Then Hitler moved against Czechoslovakia in early 1939 and annexed the remainder of it in March. The agreement lasted only six months.

Source: Public Domain

No Foreign Entanglements

Historically, harking back to George Washington, the United States maintained a policy of non-intervention in world affairs, which led to a strong isolationist movement in America during the late 1930s. This sentiment made it difficult to increase military spending to counter Germany's and Japan's growing aggression.

Source: Public Domain

Poland Invaded – 1939

Germany invaded Poland on September 1, 1939. On September 3rd, France and England declared war on the Nazi state. It ignited another world war the two Allied countries had worked hard to avoid.

Source: Public Domain

The West Invaded – 1940

In April 1940 Hitler invaded Denmark and Norway, quickly conquering both nations. On May 10, 1940, the German dictator launched Blitzkrieg (lightning war) on western Europe overrunning the Netherlands, Belgium and much of France by June 1940.

Source: Public Domain

German Weaponry

New German weapons spearheaded the Wehrmacht's victories in Poland and the West. The Panzer Mark IV tank represented Germany's superiority in weapons and Blitzkrieg their advantages in tactics.

Source: Ausf C. Attribution: Bundesarchiv, Bild 183-J08365 / CC-BY-SA

United States Weaponry

By the late 1930s, the United States lagged far behind Germany in weapons development. The MI Light Tank represented the inferiority of American weapons to those of the Germans. America would need major advances in its arsenal to compete on the battlefield with the Wehrmacht.

Source: Public Domain

German Victory

German troops marched unopposed into Paris on June 14, 1940. On June 22, 1940, France signed an armistice that represented their full surrender to Germany. Great Britain now stood alone to fight the Nazi onslaught.

Source: Bundesarchiv, Bild 101I-126-0347-09A / Gutjahr / CC-BY-SA

CHAPTER 2

The American Bantam Car Company

Sources (main): George Edward Domer, Automotive Quarterly, Fall 1976; (inserts): John W. Underwood, Heritage Press, 1965

Sir Herbert Austin

A successful pioneer in the development of small cars in Europe during the early part of the 20th century, Sir Herbert Austin would attempt to bring those vehicles to the United States.

Source: Alamy Ltd.

The 1937 Austin 7

Sir Herbert created the Austin 7 in the early 1920s and the small car proved immensely popular in Europe with its short driving distances and high gasoline prices. He would attempt to bring vehicles such as this to America.

Source: Public Domain {PD-1996}

Main Street, Butler, Pennsylvania

Sir Herbert Austin began his quest to sell small cars in the United States in Butler, PA, due to the availability of an idle automobile factory in that city.

Source: Photo Courtesy of the Butler County Historical Society

The American Austin Car Company

Sir Herbert founded the American Austin Car Company in Butler in 1929. However, the economic disaster of the Great Depression and Americans' lack of interest in small cars led to lackluster sales.

Source: Public Domain

The 1931 American Austin Roadster

A slick and stylish small car the American Austin Roadster proved unpopular in the United States. However, this vehicle, its predecessor the Austin 7 and its successor, the American Bantam Roadster, formed the lineage from which the first Jeep came into being.

Source: Photo used with permission from Dale Lynn James.

1932 American Austin Roadster

The updated model of the 1931 version of this vehicle, or one like it, found its way into the hands of the United States Army. While proving unsatisfactory for military use, parts from that vehicle would find their way into a forerunner of the Jeep.

Source: Used by permission from sportscarmarket.com

Roy S. Evans

The American Austin Car Company went bankrupt in the early 1930s. In 1935 an entrepreneur named Roy Evans purchased the remains of Sir Herbert's company and tried again to manufacture and sell small cars into the American market. Roy Evans is pictured in the passenger seat of a Bantam Roadster circa the late 1930s.

Source: John W. Underwood, Heritage Press, 1965

1911 Maxwell Touring Car

Roy Evans displayed a knack for entrepreneurship at a young age. Born in Bartow, Georgia in 1900, by age of 14 he ran a taxi business from a Maxwell touring car, shepherding citizens around his hometown.

Source: Public Domain

1920s Model T Ford

In the early 1920s, Evans purchased his first car, a Model T Ford. He immediately fell in love with the automobile industry and would work in that field for the next twenty years of his life.

Source: Public Domain

American Bantam Car Company

After Evans purchased the assets of the American Austin Car Company, he assembled a team to bring small cars to America. He used the term Bantam in the name because the Austins had acquired that nickname, a reference to miniature chickens applied to Austin's diminutive vehicles.

Bantam Factory Building. Source: Photo Courtesy of the Butler County Historical Society

American Bantam Struggles

Though offering a superb line of cars, Evans' vehicles failed to gain a foothold in the American market. In addition, a "deep recession within the Great Depression" made sales even more difficult to come by.

Bantam Logo drawing by Manuel Freedman

American Bantam on the Ropes

Sales plummeted in 1938, which forced Evans and his team to seek a loan underwritten by the Federal Government and obtained from the Reconstruction Finance Corporation. These funds helped to keep the floundering firm afloat until its rendezvous with destiny in 1940.

Source: Public Domain

1940 American Bantam Roadster Convertible

By early 1940 Bantam had innovated small cars as far as they could. Yet the firm, like its predecessor, found itself bankrupt. Unless a miracle occurred, the firm would end up in the dustbin of history, forgotten by later generations.

Source: Used by permission from Conceptcarz.com

CHAPTER 3

Genesis of a Legend

The mule symbolized the U.S. Army's need to modernize in the 1930s. Source: Public Domain

Mule and Motorcycle with Sidecar

Even in the late 1930s the U.S. Army still relied on the mule for carrying troops and small payloads. This proved obsolete in World War I. The motorcycle with sidecar did not perform well in difficult or cross-country terrain. The U.S military needed a completely new vehicle to wage war in the 20th century.

U.S. Army tests a motorcycle with sidecar, 1917. Source: Public Domain

Early Small Vehicle Concept

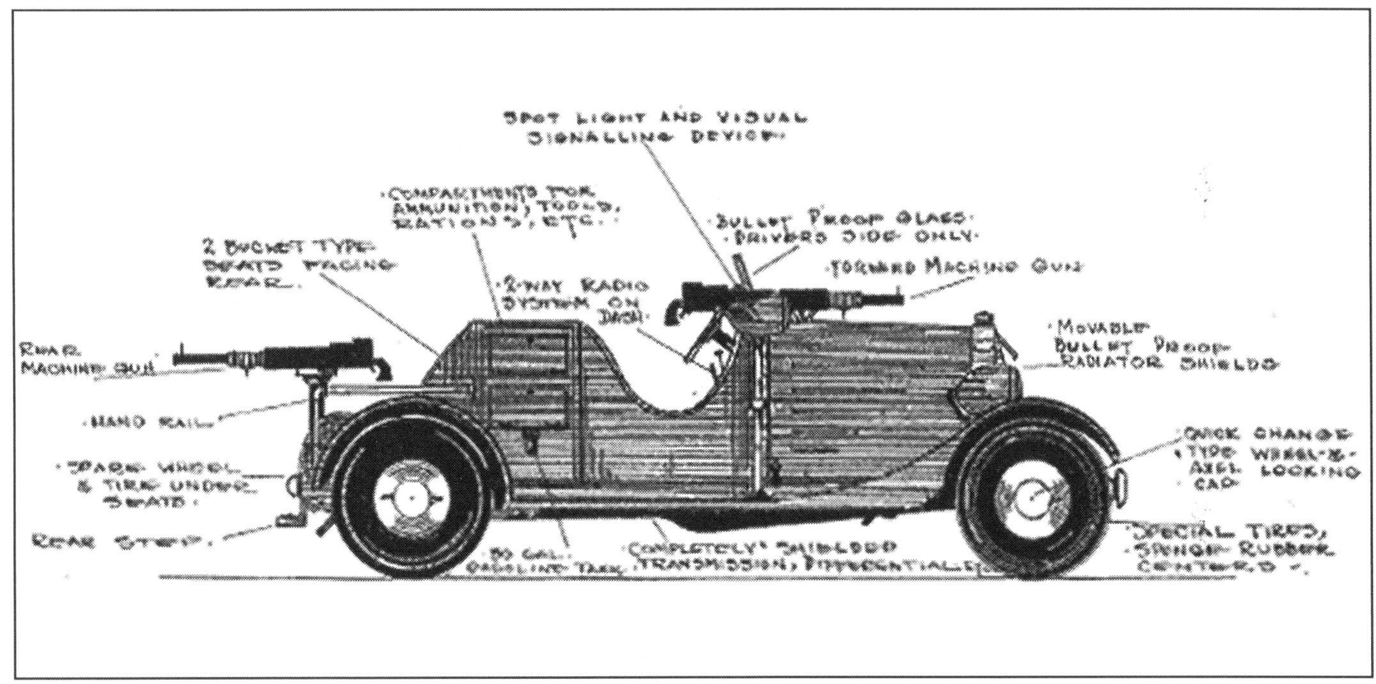

In 1935, a Colonel by the name of Hamilton proposed a light vehicle for Cavalry purposes. This demonstrated that by the mid-1930s the U.S. Army knew it needed something much more suitable and substantial than the mule and the motorcycle with sidecar.

Source: United States National Archives, College Park, Maryland

The Howie Carrier (1of 2)

In April 1937 the Infantry attempted to create a vehicle needed to replace the mule and motorcycle with sidecar. The Army named the contraption the Howie Machine Gun Carrier after Captain Robert G. Howie, who led the team that built it.

Source: Public Domain

The Howie Carrier (2 of 2)

The Infantry extensively evaluated and tested the Howie Carrier. At the time it seemed possible it could provide the solution to fulfill the Infantry's needs, but subsequent events would prove otherwise. In an ironic twist, Captain Howie used salvaged parts in his vehicle from a 1932 Austin.

Source: Public Domain

The Marmon-Herrington 4X4 Truck

The Infantry conducted numerous tests on commercial vehicles during the late 1930s. In 1938 they settled upon the Marmon-Herrington 1/2-ton 4x4 truck. However, that branch, working through the Quartermaster Corp., could not obtain a suitable vehicle.

Source: Public Domain

The Bantam Chassis Test

27

c. A test run conducted after the break-in period, using a measured quantity of fuel with vehicle operating on a level concrete road carrying two passengers gave a mileage of 24.4 miles to the gallon. Regular issue gasoline was used.

d. There were no maintenance costs other than those incident to installing new main bearing and fly wheel and making minor adjustments. No parts were worn out or broken during the test.

4. RESULTS OF THE TEST.--The test indicated that:

a. The vehicle has little unimproved road or cross country mobility. Difficulty was experienced in climbing grades encountered when vehicle was carrying two passengers. There was insufficient power and flotation to permit operation over muddy clay roads.

b. The vehicle cannot perform the missions of the motorcycle for the reason that it accelerates too slowly, and cannot quickly attain the speed desired. It is less flexible than a motorcycle due to its greater turning radius.

c. The narrow gauge of the vehicle makes operation on clay roads difficult as car must be driven straddle of one rut or with outside wheels in one rut.

d. The cargo capacity of the vehicle (one-fourth ton) is generally too small to permit of its use as a weapon carrier, as transportation of a machine gun with ammunition and minimum crew usually results in an overload.

e. The vehicle generally lacks the power, ability to accelerate and mobility necessary in any tactical vehicle with cavalry.

5. CONCLUSIONS.--The Cavalry Board, therefore, concludes that the subject vehicle is not suitable for any tactical use in cavalry, either horse or mechanized.

6. RECOMMENDATIONS.--The board recommends that the Bantam chassis be considered unsuitable for any tactical uses in cavalry either horse or mechanized.

For the President:

Dorsey R. Rodney
Dorsey R. Rodney,
Colonel, Cavalry,
Director.
27

6. RECOMMENDATIONS.--The board recommends that the Bantam chassis be considered unsuitable for any tactical uses in cavalry either horse or mechanized.

- 2 -

Bantam furnished a chassis for testing by the Calvary in 1938. The result, "the board recommends that the Bantam chassis be considered unsuitable for any tactical uses in cavalry either horse or mechanized."

Source: United States National Archives, College Park, Maryland

The Bantam Truck

1937 AMERICAN BANTAM PICK-UP TRUCK

This open-bodied truck will carry a quarter-ton load. The rear gate opens for easy loading. Comes also equipped with stakes and tarpaulin cover frame. The driver's cab is completely enclosed. The chassis price is $275. Chassis with pick-up body is $385. Prices are F.O.B. Butler, Pa.

Bantam furnished a truck to the Infantry in 1938 for evaluation. The result, "the Bantam 1/4-ton truck proved to be entirely unsuitable for use as a cross-country carrier and no requirement is known for Infantry use of this vehicle. This vehicle lacks adequate power, performance and capacity for use as a cross-country carrier."

Source: Public Domain

Fenn 1939 Letter

EXECUTIVE OFFICES
AMERICAN BANTAM CAR COMPANY
BUTLER, PA.
U.S.A.

September 25, 1939

Lt. Col. H. C. Lawes, Q.M.C.
Holabird Quartermaster Depot
Baltimore, Maryland

Sir:

Some months ago this company made the error of selling three Bantam chasses to the Quartermaster Corps for trial, which was a serious mistake inasmuch as these cars in no way came up to the government requirements -- in fact they were the first series of cars manufactured by this company and had I been connected with the company at that time I would not have permitted the sale. Since then, however, our entire unit has been redesigned and our 1940 models will, in my opinion, provide anything and everything demanded for army use up to their carrying capacity. The present car is equipped with a three-bearing engine with 25% more horsepower than those originally used. They are equipped with two-way springs and hydraulic shock absorbers. The frame has been strengthened and the radius rod assembly in the front end has been greatly strengthened. These cars will go over hills any place within a hundred-mile radius of Butler at speeds of 45 miles to 60 miles per hour, fully loaded. The speed on level ground is 70 miles per hour. It is possible to put them through the gears from a dead stop up to 30 miles an hour in 30 seconds. Our new self-equalizing brakes stop these cars in twice their own length from 30 miles an hour. They use no oil and the gallonage consumed in ordinary work is from 40 to 50 miles per gallon.

I am sure if you will look up the records of the old car, you will decide that there is nothing about these to which the old one could be compared and the thing we are after, Colonel, is an opportunity to demonstrate these cars to you again at our expense.

During the Maneuvers at Manassas, Majors Eggers and Leetch used one of these cars for reconaissance purposes and found them far more satisfactory than a motorcycle and sidecar. They could go anywhere the foregoing vehicle could go and many places where they could not because of their power. The use of these cars is in no way confined to highways. They followed marching troops everywhere, over any trail which the troops chanced to follow. The cars were extremely well liked with the result that Major Eggers has given me your name, together with several others in the War Department, in the Quartermaster Corps, because he is of the opinion that there is a definite place for our equipment in the service.

After Bantam's rejection by both the Cavalry and Infantry, Frank Fenn, the company President, wrote to the Quartermaster in an attempt to gain another chance for the Army to consider their vehicles.

Source: United States National Archives, College Park, MD

Army Response to Fenn's Letter

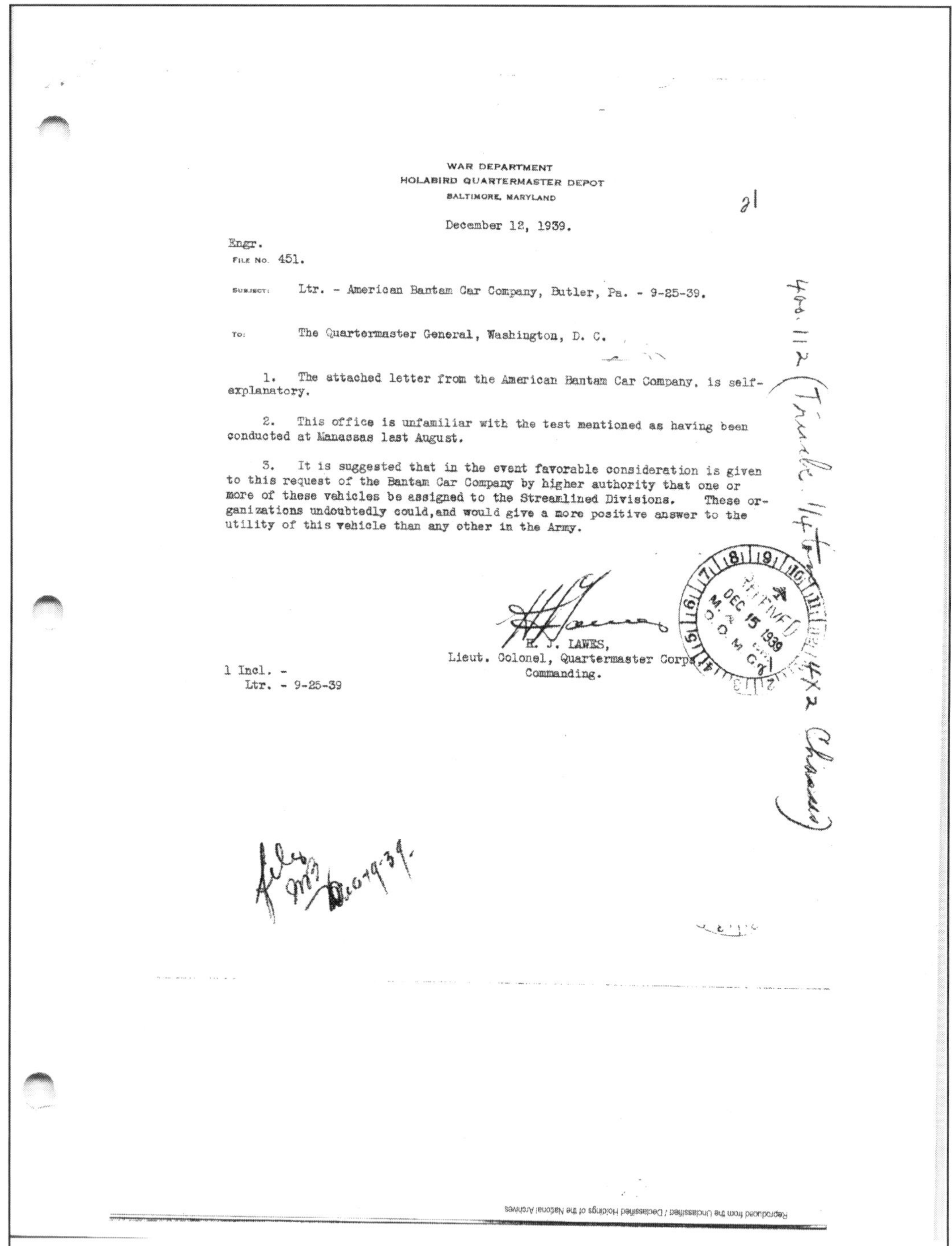

WAR DEPARTMENT
HOLABIRD QUARTERMASTER DEPOT
BALTIMORE, MARYLAND

December 12, 1939.

Engr.
FILE No. 451.

SUBJECT: Ltr. - American Bantam Car Company, Butler, Pa. - 9-25-39.

TO: The Quartermaster General, Washington, D. C.

1. The attached letter from the American Bantam Car Company, is self-explanatory.

2. This office is unfamiliar with the test mentioned as having been conducted at Manassas last August.

3. It is suggested that in the event favorable consideration is given to this request of the Bantam Car Company by higher authority that one or more of these vehicles be assigned to the Streamlined Divisions. These organizations undoubtedly could, and would give a more positive answer to the utility of this vehicle than any other in the Army.

H. J. LAWES,
Lieut. Colonel, Quartermaster Corps,
Commanding.

1 Incl. -
Ltr. - 9-25-39

Lt. Colonel H. J. Lawes, who would play a considerable role in the Jeep's development, responded to Fenn's request by relegating Bantam to the "Streamlined Divisions". The door for the Butler company's attempt to sell vehicles to the Army closed yet again.

Source: United States National Archives, College Park, Maryland

CHAPTER 4

What Do We Want?

WAR DEPARTMENT
OFFICE OF THE CHIEF OF INFANTRY
WASHINGTON

CI 470.8/550 XII "C"

June 6, 1940

Subject: Light Vehicle Development.

To: The Adjutant General
(THROUGH The Chief of Cavalry)

1. Facilities available to organizations for increased speed in tactical employment of infantry units, including development of more rapid means of communication within the infantry battalion, demand greater mobility for platoon leaders of the Heavy Weapons Company and cross-country ability for motorcycle messengers.

2. The command and reconnaissance car used by the company commander and platoon leaders of the Heavy Weapons Company is a much larger vehicle than is required by subordinate leaders. It is, moreover, unsuitable because of its weight and relatively high silhouette. A light and less expensive vehicle, capable of being manhandled by two men, is much more desirable. The nature of the duties of the company and platoon commanders in combat which involves movement in close proximity to an opposing force, requires a vehicle of the minimum silhouette.

In the motorization of the Heavy Weapons Company the effort was made to provide a vehicle which would take the place of the horse with which the officers were formerly mounted. A vehicle of small capacity would fulfil this purpose.

3. The motorcycle now issued to organizations is suitable for traffic control and messenger service, but efficient operation of it is limited to roads and improved trails. It is not well suited to cross-country movement.

4. To meet this situation a requirement is set up by the infantry for a vehicle of the following approximate characteristics:

a. Maximum height: 36 inches.

b. Maximum weight, without pay load: 750-1000 lbs.

17

June 6, 1940 memo that started Jeep procurement. Source: U.S Nat. Archives, College Park, Maryland

Invasion of Denmark and Norway

On April 9, 1940, Hitler launched an invasion of Denmark and Norway in a prelude to his attack in the west to come the following month. Denmark surrendered quickly. Norway resisted the invasion but eventually surrendered on June 10, 1940.

Source: Public Domain

Frank Fenn

Frank Fenn became President of the American Bantam Car Company in 1939. He would provide the executive leadership for Bantam's attempt to provide a small reconnaissance car to the United States Army.

Photo was pasted into a scrapbook that was presented to Fenn by his employees in 1943.
Source: Photographer Unknown, assumed Public Domain

Charles H. Payne

Fenn hired Charles Payne in early 1940 to spearhead Bantam's efforts to secure government contracts. A pioneering naval aviator during WW I, his eclectic background included selling Avro training planes to the Mexican government in the 1920s.

Source: Public Domain

Payne's Small Rescue Car

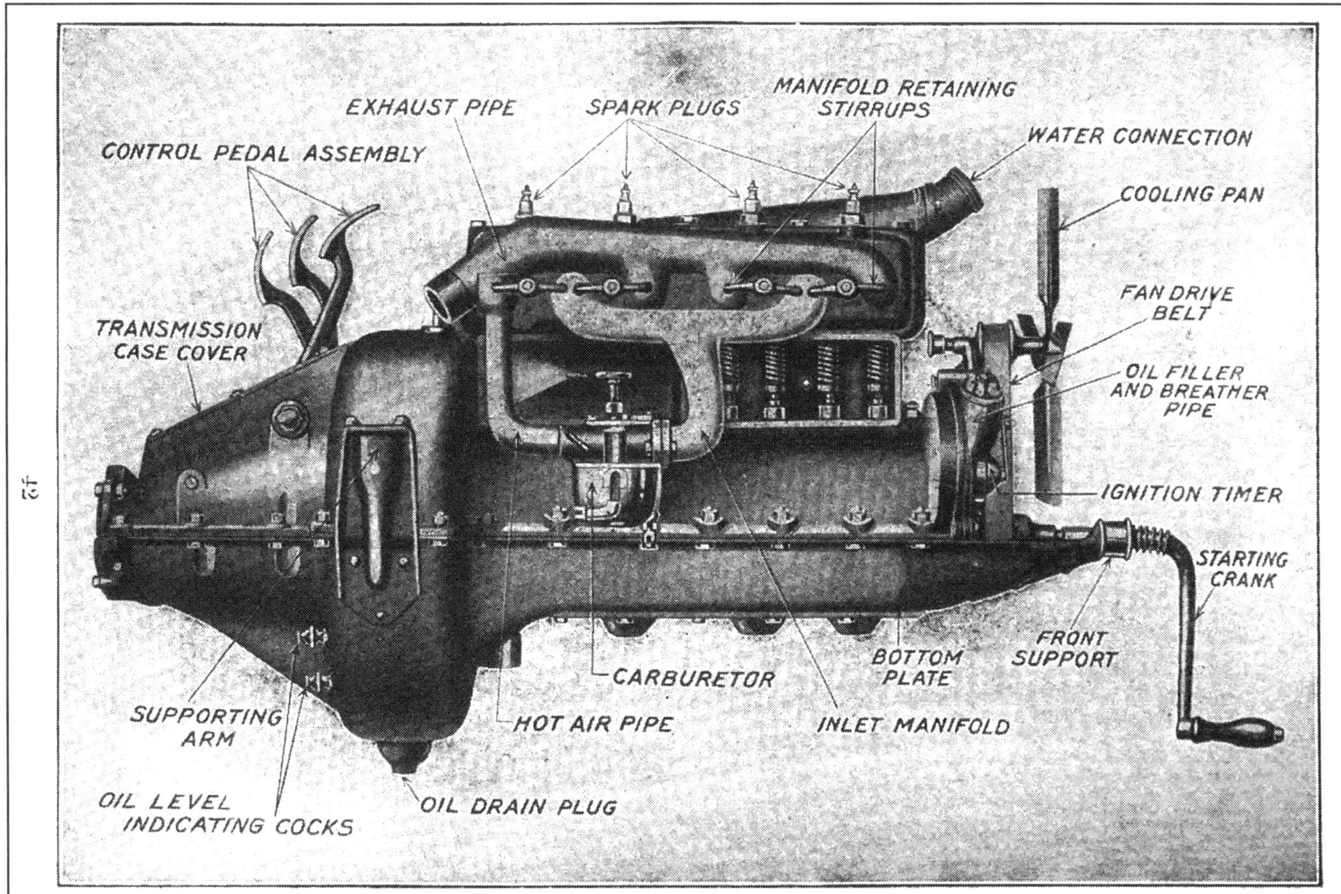

Fig. 8.—Valve Side of the Ford Model T Unit Power Plant Showing Manifolds, Carburetor and Interior of One of the Valve Spring Chambers.

During the 1920s, Payne trained pilots, hazardous work which led to frequent crashes in remote areas. To facilitate rescuing downed pilots, Payne created a "small rescue car" using Ford parts. This gave him experience in designing small vehicles that operated in difficult conditions.

Source: Public Domain

Invasion in the West—May 1940

On May 10, 1940, Germany invaded Luxembourg, Belgium, and the Netherlands. These nations were no match for the Wehrmacht and quickly capitulated. Hitler also invaded France that day, which held out until June 22, 1940.

Source: Public Domain

Colonel Ingomar M. Oseth

Colonel Ingomar Oseth served in the Infantry branch of the United States Army and had an extensive background in what type of vehicles that each branch of the using arms needed. He would play an extensive role in the Jeep's development.

Source: Public Domain

The May 1940 Camp Holabird Conference

In late May 1940, while Germany continued overrunning Western Europe, a conference took place near Baltimore, Maryland, at Camp Holabird, the Army's main vehicle procurement center from 1917 to 1972. This base would serve as the Army's focal point in the Jeep's development.

Source: Library of Congress. Public Domain

Oseth Meets Payne

At the aforementioned Holabird conference, the attendees concluded that the Army did not have a light vehicle that could match up to the Germans. Nor did they have any plans to develop one. On May 20, 1940, Oseth returned to his office and found Charles Payne, "...who was sitting in the window behind my chair!"

Source: Library of Congress. Public Domain

British Army Evacuated at Dunkirk

By late May 1940, the Germans had surrounded the British Army in France at Dunkirk. Through an incredible series of events, the force evacuated to Britain, but their departure left the French to fight the Germans alone. English troops would not return to the continent for four years.

Source: Public Domain

Infantry Develops General Specs

After their initial meeting on May 20, 1940, Oseth and Payne would develop specifications for a light vehicle over the next few weeks that would meet the Infantry's needs. A low silhouette like the 1939 Bantam Roadster had comprised a key feature needed in the vehicle.

Source: Public Domain

The June 6, 1940, Memo Developed

After agreeing on a general set of vehicle characteristics, Oseth wrote a memo first in pencil, then typed it up both in rough and final draft for signature by his superior. The memo would request that the Adjutant General approve a vehicle procurement which met the specifications in the memo.

Source: Public Domain

The June 6, 1940, Memo, Page 1

WAR DEPARTMENT
OFFICE OF THE CHIEF OF INFANTRY
WASHINGTON

CI 470.8/550 XII "C"

June 6, 1940

Subject: Light Vehicle Development.

To: The Adjutant General
(THROUGH The Chief of Cavalry)

1. Facilities available to organizations for increased speed in tactical employment of infantry units, including development of more rapid means of communication within the infantry battalion, demand greater mobility for platoon leaders of the Heavy Weapons Company and cross-country ability for motorcycle messengers.

2. The command and reconnaissance car used by the company commander and platoon leaders of the Heavy Weapons Company is a much larger vehicle than is required by subordinate leaders. It is, moreover, unsuitable because of its weight and relatively high silhouette. A light and less expensive vehicle, capable of being manhandled by two men, is much more desirable. The nature of the duties of the company and platoon commanders in combat which involves movement in close proximity to an opposing force, requires a vehicle of the minimum silhouette.

In the motorization of the Heavy Weapons Company the effort was made to provide a vehicle which would take the place of the horse with which the officers were formerly mounted. A vehicle of small capacity would fulfil this purpose.

3. The motorcycle now issued to organizations is suitable for traffic control and messenger service, but efficient operation of it is limited to roads and improved trails. It is not well suited to cross-country movement.

4. To meet this situation a requirement is set up by the infantry for a vehicle of the following approximate characteristics:

a. Maximum height: 36 inches.

b. Maximum weight, without pay load: 750-1000 lbs.

17

14

The June 6, 1940 Memo lit the fuse for all the events that led to the Jeep's development. The first page describes the need for the vehicle and begins the list of requirements.

Source: United States National Archives, College Park, Maryland

The June 6, 1940, Memo, Page 2

c. Adequate cross-country ability and gradeability equal to that of standard cargo vehicles.

d. Caliber .30 machine gun mount either integral with the body of the vehicle or detachable.

e. Capacity: a crew of at least two men, one machine gun with accessories, and three thousand rounds of ammunition or equivalent weight.

f. Armored face shield for driver.

g. Four-wheel drive (except where tricycles are considered).

h. Ground clearance: maximum possible consistent with desired silhouette.

5. If feasible, without unduly delaying production of test vehicles, it is desirable that the frame and body be so designed as to provide amphibian characteristics. If it is not feasible under present conditions to incorporate this feature, it is desirable that experimentation and development along that line continue with a view to its ultimate inclusion.

6. The Chief of Infantry recommends that the proper agency be directed to procure, without delay, a sufficient number of vehicles conforming generally to the above characteristics, to equip an infantry regiment (rifle) with such vehicles in lieu of standard command and reconnaissance trucks for company units, with 6 additional for the Infantry Board (or a total of 40) for extended field test in comparison with the present standard vehicles.

7. Since the desired type of vehicle is a special one, and since experience has shown the impracticability of securing development of the proper type of vehicle from among present commercial types, it is recommended that requirements for competitive bidding be waived to the extent necessary to bring about procurement of the best possible design.

For the Chief of Infantry:

E. W. FALES,
Lieutenant Colonel, Infantry,
Executive.

REC'D.
JUN 8 1940
O. C. CAV.

16

15

-2-

The second page of the memo completes the requirements and requests, "that the proper agency be directed to procure without delay, a sufficient number of vehicles conforming generally to the above characteristics." The search for a solution to the vexing problem of a light vehicle had begun.

Source: United States National Archives, College Park, Maryland

Oseth's "Lawyer's Trick"

Colonel Oseth later testified that he included a requirement for an armored face-shield for the driver. Due to frustrations with the Quartermaster Corps, which normally handled this type of procurement, with his "lawyer's trick", as he referred to it, he wanted instead to steer the effort to the Ordnance Branch. Ordnance would decide the next steps in the effort.

Source: Public Domain

Harold Crist Intro

A skilled draftsman and mechanical genius, Harold Crist, Bantam's Plant Manager, played an integral role in the Jeep's development. The former Stutz employee would begin his contribution shorty after the release of the June 6th memo and continued through the development of the specifications. Ultimately he led the team that hand-built the first Jeep.

1912 Stutz Racer. Source: Public Domain

CHAPTER 5

A Vehicle Takes Shape

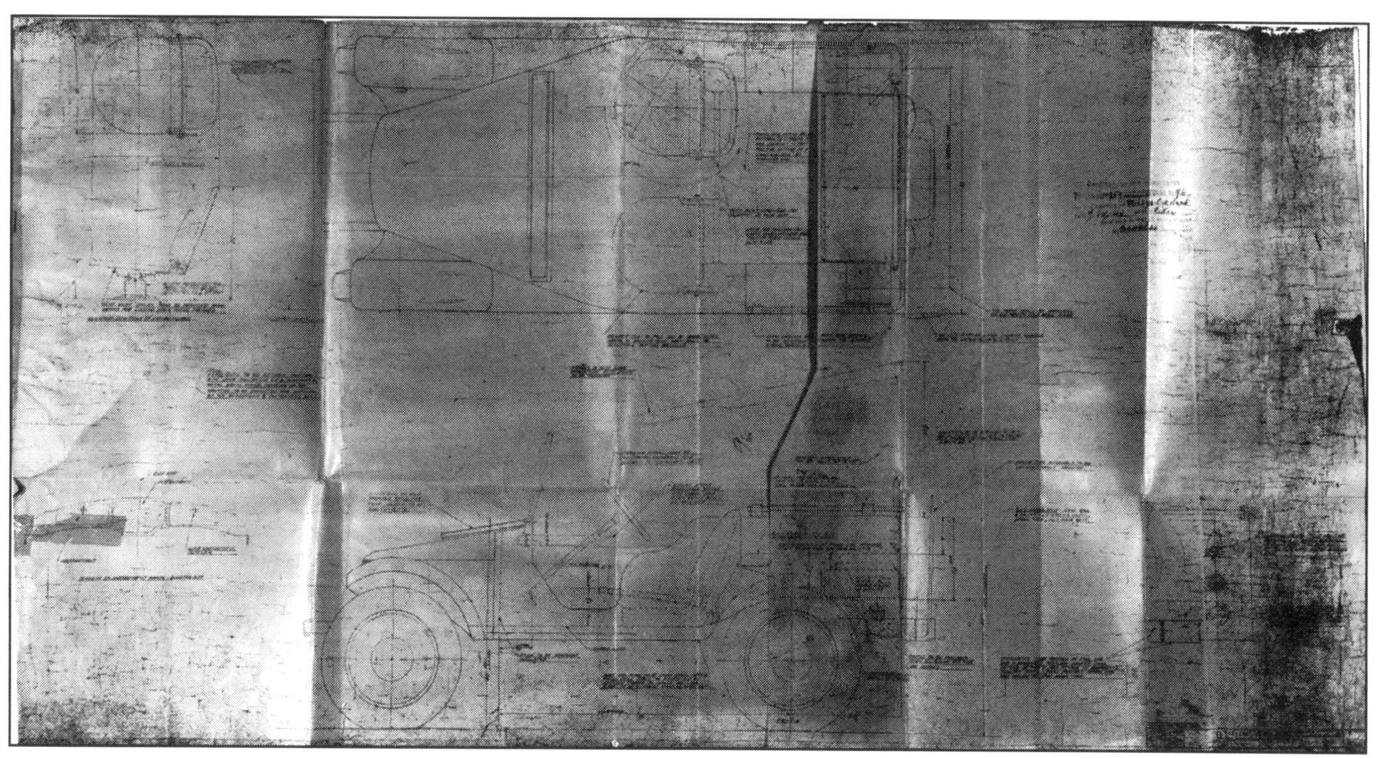

Body Assembly Drawing - 08370-Z. Source: United States National Archives, College Park, Maryland

Memo Routed to Ordnance & QMC

451 1st Ind.

War Department, Office Chief of Cavalry, Washington, D. C., June 8, 1940.
To: The Adjutant General.

The Chief of Cavalry is interested in the possibility of using a light, cheap car for command and reconnaissance purposes in the cavalry. He therefore concurs in the recommendations of the Chief of Infantry in the basic communication and recommends that he be kept informed of the development and that twenty cars, when manufactured, be made available to him for test.

20 cars

For the Chief of Cavalry:

K. S. Bradford
Colonel, Cavalry
Executive

JUN 8
Received

29365-64
G-4 JUN

15

SUBJECT: Light Vehicle Development.

AG 451 2nd Ind. FBD/et
(6-6-40) M-D

War Dept., A.G.O., June 14,1940 - To The Quartermaster General AND the Chief of Ordnance, IN TURN.

For comment and recommendation.

By order of the Secretary of War:

Adjutant General.

The infantry routed the June 6, 1940 memo through the Cavalry to obtain further support for the procurement. Once he received the memo, the Adjutant General sent it to the Ordnance and Quartermaster for review.

Source: United States National Archives, College Park, Maryland

QMC Wants In

QM 451 T-M 3rd Ind.

War Department, OQMG, Washington, June 14, 1940. - To Commanding Officer, Holabird Quartermaster Depot, Baltimore, Md.

1. In view of the fact that the vehicle is required for command-reconnaissance purposes as well as for combat purposes, it is considered that the chassis development should be a responsibility of the Quartermaster Corps. Comment is requested as to the practicability of securing a commercial vehicle with all wheel drive conversion, meeting the vehicle characteristics set up in the basic communication. The light passenger car of the American Bantam Company is suggested as a possible solution of the problem.

For The Quartermaster General:

J. H. JOHNSON,
Lieut. Colonel, Q. M. C.,
Assistant.

14

12

On June 14, 1940, the Quartermaster Corp. responded. Because they represented the using arm that obtained items for the Army, they believed they should play a substantial role in the procurement. Stunningly the QMC stated, "the light passenger car of the American Bantam Company is suggested as a possible solution..."

Source: United States National Archives, College Park, Maryland

AG Directs Ordnance

REFER TO

WASHINGTON June 15, 1940.

Subject: Light Vehicle Development.

To: The Chief of Ordnance.

1. In view of the fact that the Chief of Ordnance is being directed, in a separate communication, to give further consideration to the Howie Experimental Weapons Carrier, the attached copy of a letter to this office, regarding proposed military characteristics of a vehicle for Infantry use, is forwarded for appropriate action and recommendation through the Ordnance Technical Committee.

2. In this connection it is desired that consideration be given to the possible use of the American Bantam car manufactured by the American Bantam Company, Butler, Pa.

3. It is further desired that the subcommitted appointed to investigate this matter include, in addition to those members of the Ordnance Technical Committee you wish to designate, a representative of each of the following arms and services:

Chief of Infantry (Lt. Col. Lee)
Chief of Cavalry (Maj. Tompkins)
The Quartermaster General (such representatives as he may wish to designate).

4. You are authorized to request travel orders for such members of the Ordnance subcommittee as may be necessary to conduct a thorough investigation into this matter, and to confer with officials of the automobile industry in the development of a vehicle possessing the desired characteristics.

5. Your recommendations are desired at the earliest practicable date.

By order of the Secretary of War:

Adjutant General.

1 incl.
Copy of letter.

1.

IMMEDIATE ACTION

On June 15, 1940, the Adjutant General directed Ordnance to set up a committee to handle the matter. It was to include members of Infantry and Cavalry. The AG also authorized travel funds if needed in the "investigation into this matter".

Source: United States National Archives, College Park, Maryland

Ordnance Tech Committee Meets

War Department
Office of the Chief of Ordnance

Project OK.
T.S.T.P.

Item
June 17, 1940
Date

From: Sub-Committee on Automotive.

To: The Ordnance Committee, Technical Staff

Subject: LIGHT INFANTRY VEHICLES - Development of.

1. REFERENCES:

a. O.O. 455.6/624, including report of Infantry Board.

b. Letter dated June 6, 1940, from The Chief of Infantry to The Adjutant General, through the Chief of Cavalry, with 1st, 2nd, and 3rd indorsements thereon; subject: Light Vehicle Development.

c. O.O. 451/10001, letter from The Adjutant General to the Chief of Ordnance dated June 15, 1940, Subject: Light Vehicle Development.

2. DISCUSSION:

a. From a consideration of the above references, the Subcommittee concludes that two types of vehicles are under consideration:

1. The Light Command and Reconnaissance Car.

2. The Howie Weapons Carrier.

b. The Light Command and Reconnaissance Car represents a new type of vehicle, the proposed military characteristics of which are stated by the Chief of Infantry in reference b. The Subcommittee feels that these military characteristics are satisfactory, in general, but will give them further study at the conference to be held at the American Bantam Company's plant.

c. The letter of instructions from The Adjutant General to the Chief of Ordnance (reference c.) refers in par. 1 to instructions to the Chief of Ordnance in regard to further consideration of the Howie

34

MCN

The committee met on June 17, 1940. In the running were a new light car and the Howie Carrier. The key decision made in this meeting: "the Subcommittee will visit the plant of the American Bantam Company [...] on Wednesday, June 19, 1940".

Source: United States National Archives, College Park, Maryland

Butler, PA—June 19, 1940

The Ordnance committee visited American Bantam on June 19, 1940. During the visit, the group went to the Butler County Fairgrounds and raced some Bantams around the track to see what they could do.

Source: Photo Courtesy of the Butler County Historical Society

The Sandbags Test

Harkening back to 1938, when the Cavalry rejected their chassis, Bantam loaded 4,500 pounds of sandbags onto one of their chassis to "show that it could take it."

Source: United States National Archives, College Park, Maryland

The Beasley-Brown Drawing

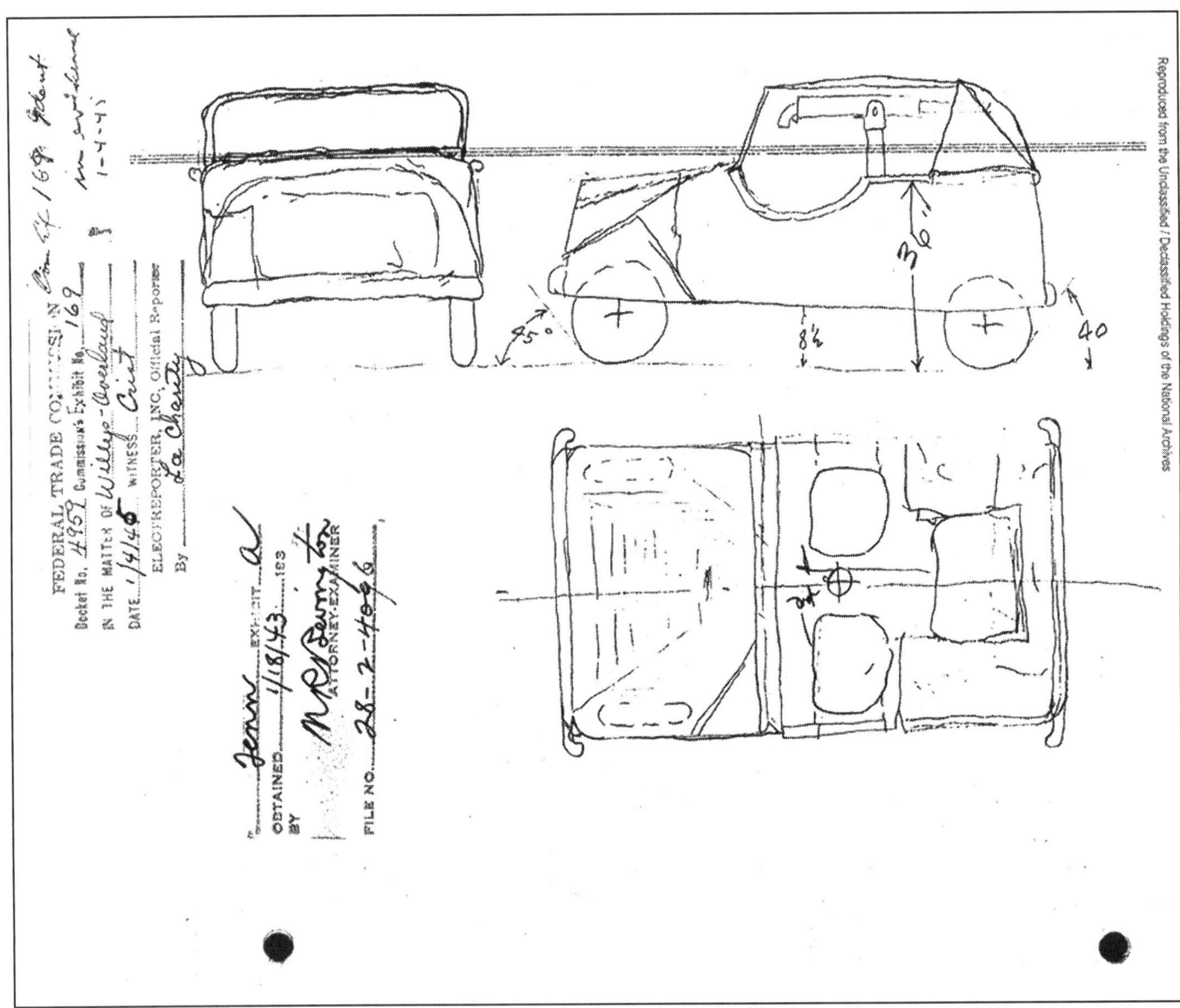

At the end of the day on June 19, 1940, the group met in Frank Fenn's office to discuss the Army's requirements. After their discussion, participants Mr. Brown and Mr. Beasley drew a concept sketch for the car. It represents the first-ever drawing of a Jeep-type vehicle.

Source: United States National Archives, College Park, Maryland

The Front Axle

Four-wheel drive became one of the critical components for the new vehicle. In 1940, only one firm could manufacture this component, Spicer Axle of Toledo, Ohio. Representatives from that firm visited Butler on June 20, 1940, to discuss this key part.

Source: United States National Archives, College Park, Maryland

Ordnance Tech Committee Meets Again

LIGHT INFANTRY AND CAVALRY VEHICLES - ~~Development of~~

(c) Maximum practicable ground clearance, but not less than 8-1/2".

(d) Cross country performance and grade ability comparable to that of standard multi-wheeled cargo vehicles.

f. The Light Reconnaissance and Command Car is essentially the same as the Howie Weapons Carrier except for the prone position of the operator. If the Howie Weapons Carrier is to operate in convoy with other vehicles, it must be equipped with conventional steering, brake and clutch controls; if it is not so equipped, it must be transported in trucks. The Subcommittee believes that the test of the Light Reconnaissance and Command Car will determine whether or not further development of the Light Reconnaissance Car and Howie Weapons Carrier should be undertaken.

3. RECOMMENDATIONS:

a. That the military characteristics stated in paragraph 2 above be approved.

b. That 70 Light Reconnaissance and Command Cars be procured for service test by Infantry, Field Artillery, and Cavalry. 40 Cars for Infantry - 20 for Cavalry and 10 for Field Artillery.

c. That since this vehicle is a commercial wheeled type without armor protection, the Quartermaster General be charged with its development and procurement.

d. That this light vehicle development be limited to the Light Reconnaissance and Command Car type, in general accordance with the military characteristics stated in paragraph 2.

e. That if this vehicle is found satisfactory, consideration be given to its use in place of the motorcycle with side car and the tricycle type of vehicle.

40

(Signatures on page 5)

RESTRICTED

-4-

The Ordnance committee met again on June 22, 1940. After much discussion five key recommendations were made – the three most important of which: more detailed military characteristics approved; authorization given to procure seventy vehicles; and the Quartermaster Corp. would lead the effort. On the third matter, Oseth's "lawyer trick" had failed.

Source: United States National Archives, College Park, Maryland

France Surrenders

France surrendered to the Germans on June 22, 1940. Great Britain now stood alone to fight the Nazi onslaught. France's capitulation to the Germans (see page 16) intensified the urgency for the United States Army to procure the new vehicle.

Source: Public Domain

Camp Holabird, Maryland

Transferring the procurement to the Quartermaster meant that coordination for the purchase would be managed from the Army's main motor transport depot, Camp Holabird, Maryland, located near Baltimore.

Source: Library of Congress. Public Domain

Colonel Edwin S. Van Deusen

The transfer of the procurement to the Quartermaster brought Colonel Edwin S. Van Deusen, the chief of Camp Holabird's engineering branch into the project. He would play a major role in the Jeep's development.

Source: Public Domain

Refining the Characteristics

From approximately June 27, 1940 to July 2, 1940, numerous individuals worked tirelessly at Camp Holabird to flesh out ever further the vehicle's characteristics. The results of their efforts, a detailed specification ES-475 and a body-assembly drawing 08370-Z.

Source: United States National Archives, College Park, Maryland

Specification ES-475

Quartermaster Corps
Tentative Specification

ES - No. 475.

July 2, 1940.

TRUCK, MOTOR GASOLINE,
LIGHT RECONNAISSANCE & COMMAND CAR
(FOUR WHEELS--FOUR WHEEL DRIVE)

A. APPLICABLE SPECIFICATIONS.

A-1. The following current specifications and drawings in effect on date of Invitation for Bids, shall form a part of this specification:

Federal Specification ZZ-T-721b, Tubes, Automobile, Inner, and Amendment No.1
Federal Specification W-B-131b, Batteries; Storage, Ignition, Lighting and Starting.
Federal Specification ZZ-T-381b, Tires; Automobile, Pneumatic, and Amendment No. 1.
RIXS Specification 114-F, Tubes; Inner, Bullet Seal, January 15, 1940.
Q.M. Specification ES - No. 422, Tool Sets; Motor Vehicle, June 5, 1940.
Q.M. Specification ES - No. 435, Oil and Fuel Tubing; Flexible Type, December 1, 1939.
Q.M. Specification ES - No. 459, General Requirements for Truck, Motor Gasoline, May 6, 1940.
Q.M. Specification ES - No. 474, Enamel Synthetic, Olive Drab, Lusterless, June 28, 1940.
Q.M. Drawing 06822-X, Vehicle Marking, March 18, 1940.
Q.M. Drawing 08235-X, Parking Lamp; Fender Mounting, May 31, 1940.
Q.M. Drawing 08236-X, Parking Lamp; Head Lamp Mounting, May 27, 1940.
Q.M. Drawing 08242-X, Service Tail and Stop and Black-out Tail Lamp, June 5, 1940.
Q.M. Drawing 08243-X, Black-out Stop and Tail Lamp, June 5, 1940.
Q.M. Drawing 08370-Z, Body Assembly, July 2, 1940.

A-2. Responsibility for obtaining copies of the latest revisions of Specifications and Drawings listed under A-1 rests with prospective bidders.

B. GENERAL.

B-1. Quartermaster Corps Specification ES - No. 459 applies.

C. SERVICE REQUIREMENTS.

C-1. General. The trucks described in this specification are intended for use as tactical vehicles by the United States Army. They will be required to transport the rated payload, which will consist of personnel and ammunition, at relatively high rates of speed over all types of roads, trails, open and rolling cross country, with the driving wheel tires, at times, equipped with tire chains, under all conditions of weather and terrain. The truck shall be of such a design and construction as to permit of its servicing, adjustment and repair, with the minimum practicable difficulty, time and tool equipment, under difficult field service conditions. The following service and detailed requirements must be fully complied with to insure that the trucks will satisfactorily perform the required functions.

- 1 -

40/872

The Quartermaster's specification contained eighteen pages of exacting detail to which a manufacturer could build a vehicle. The document references numerous drawings for parts – the most important being body assembly drawing 08370-Z.

Source: United States National Archives, College Park, Maryland

Drawing - 08370-Z

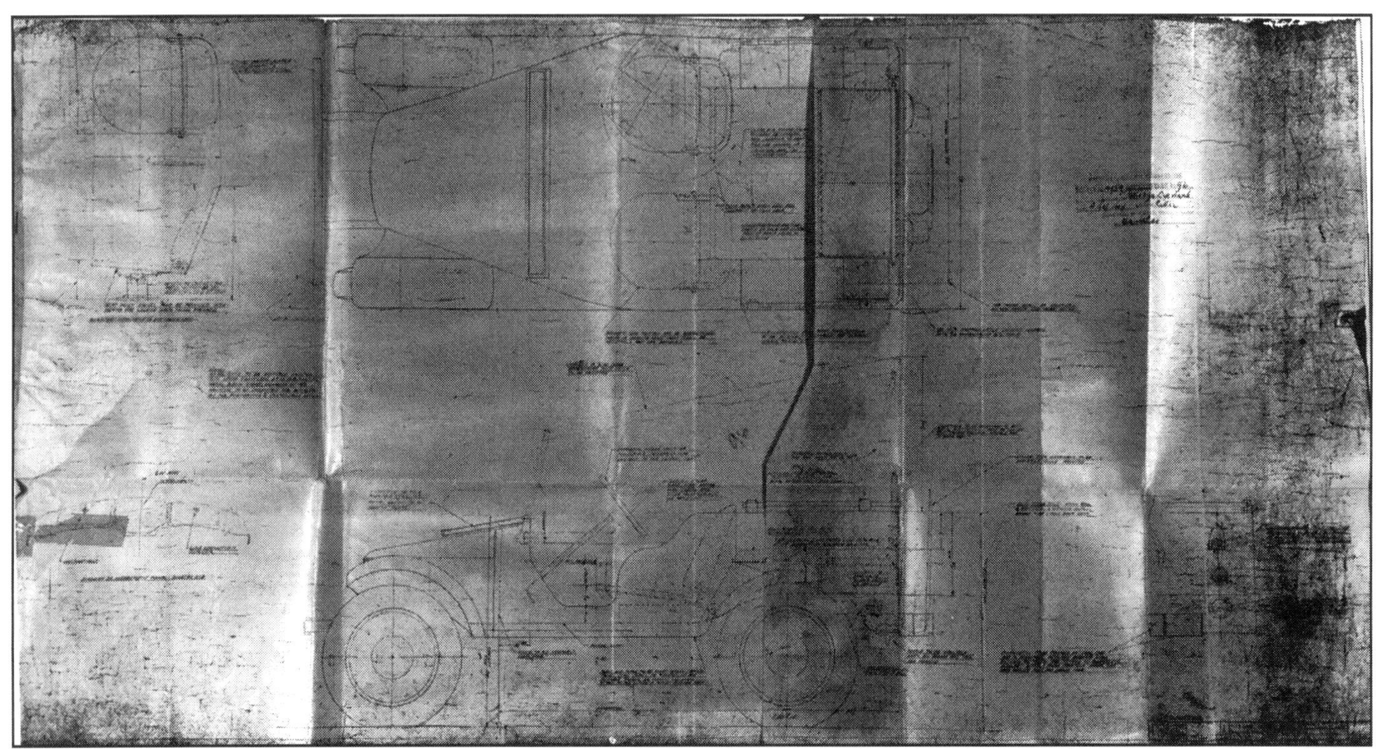

Body Assembly drawing 08370-Z reveals a significant evolution from the Beasley-Brown drawing of June 19, 1940. This drawing clearly shows a much more Jeep-like vehicle than the earlier sketch.

Source: United States National Archives, College Park, Maryland

How To Procure the Vehicle

With the drawing and specification completed, the Quartermaster now had to decide on the method for procuring the vehicle, either by negotiated contract or bid process. Their decision would lead to great drama in July 1940.

Source: Library of Congress. Public Domain

CHAPTER 6

Bidding for the First Jeep

Standard Form No. 31
Approved by the President
June 10, 1927

Invitation for Bids No. 398-41-9 Sheet No. 1a.

STANDARD GOVERNMENT FORM OF BID

(SUPPLY CONTRACT)

ORIGINAL
DUPLICATE } Indicate which by erasure
TRIPLICATE

Opening Date for this Bid

10:00 A. M., E.S.T., July 22, 1940.

To Purchasing & Contracting Officer,
Holabird Quartermaster Depot,
Baltimore, Maryland.

PLACE BUTLER, PENNSYLVANIA

DATE JULY 20, 1940

In compliance with your invitation for bids to furnish materials and supplies listed on the reverse hereof or on the accompanying schedules, numbered: Sheet No. 1b., and Q.M.C. Tentative Specification ES-No. 475, dated July 2, 1940, the undersigned, AMERICAN BANTAM CAR COMPANY

a corporation organized and existing under the laws of the State of PENNSYLVANIA
a partnership consisting of

an individual trading as

of the city of BUTLER, PENNSYLVANIA
hereby proposes to furnish, within the time specified, the materials and supplies at the prices stated opposite the respective items listed on the schedules and agrees upon receipt of written notice of the acceptance of this bid within AT ONCE days (60 days if no shorter period be specified) after the date of opening of the bids, to execute, if required, the Standard Government Form of Contract (Standard Form No. 32) in accordance with the bid as accepted, and to give bond, if required, with good and sufficient surety or sureties, for the faithful performance of the contract, within 10 days after the prescribed forms are presented for signature.

Discount will be allowed for prompt payment as follows: 10 calendar days 1% percent; 20 calendar days .... percent; 30 calendar days .... percent; or as stated in the schedules.

(Time will be computed from date of the delivery of the supplies to carrier when final inspection and acceptance are at point of origin, or from date of delivery at destination or port of embarkation when final inspection and acceptance are at those points, or from date correct bill or voucher properly certified by the contractor is received if the latter date is later than the date of delivery.)

Alex Botti
(Witness to signature)

F H Fenn
(Full name of bidder) PRESIDENT

AMERICAN BANTAM CAR COMPANY

BUTLER, PENNSYLVANIA
(Address)

NOTE.—See Standard Government Instructions to Bidders and copy of the Standard Government Form of Contract, Bid Bond, and Performance Bond, which may be obtained upon application.

To insure prompt payment bills should be certified as follows: "I certify that the above bill is correct and just and that payment therefor has not been received."

10—1803 U. S. GOVERNMENT PRINTING OFFICE (OVER)

40/869

Cover Page of Bantam's Bid Proposal. Source: United States National Archives, College Park, Maryland

Chief of Staff Approval

On June 27, 1940, a memo from the Chief of Staff of the army, George C. Marshall formally recognized the procurement. He allocated $175,000 for the effort.

Source: Public Domain

ES-475 Officially Completed

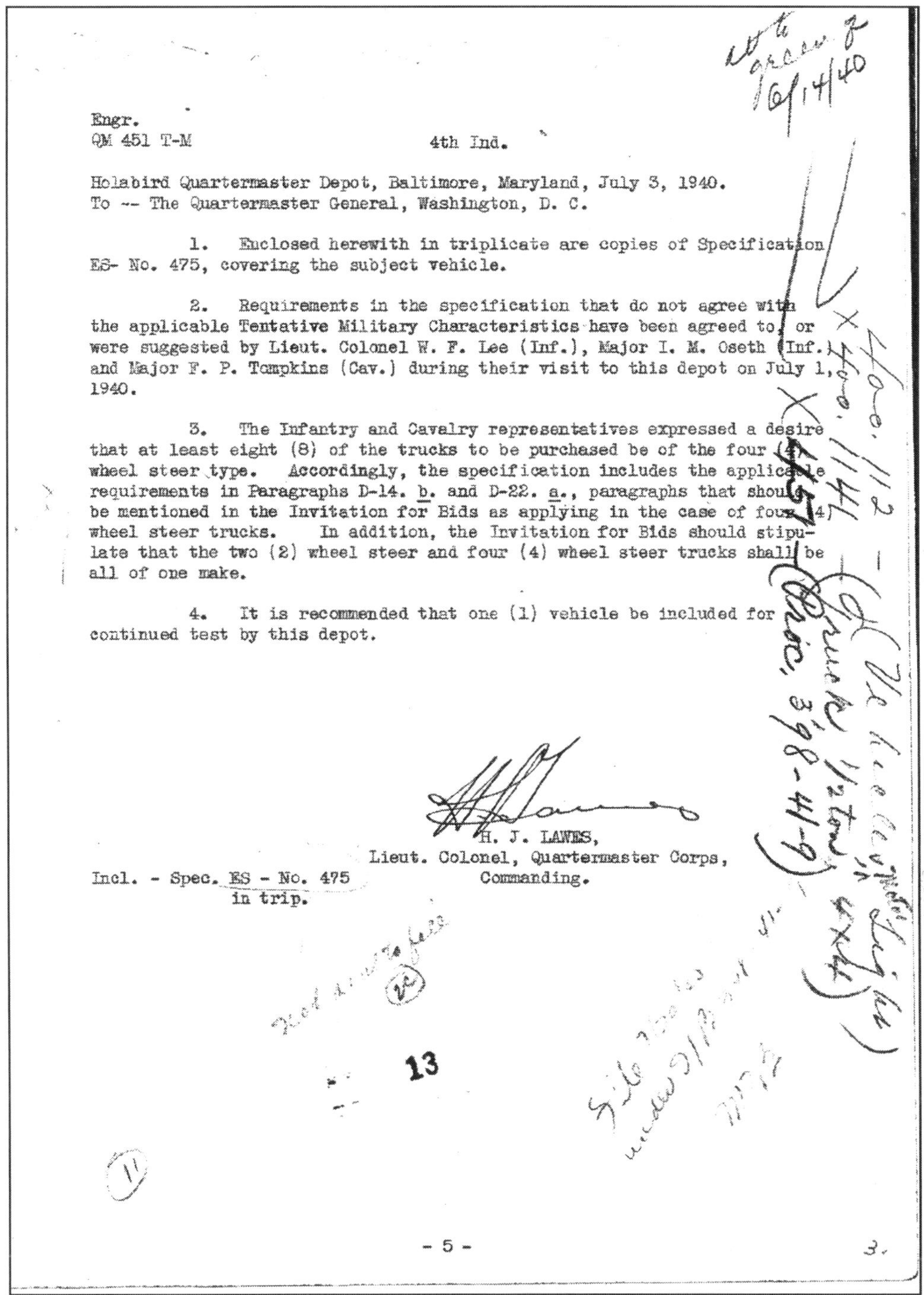

Engr.
QM 451 T-M 4th Ind.

Holabird Quartermaster Depot, Baltimore, Maryland, July 3, 1940.
To -- The Quartermaster General, Washington, D. C.

1. Enclosed herewith in triplicate are copies of Specification ES- No. 475, covering the subject vehicle.

2. Requirements in the specification that do not agree with the applicable Tentative Military Characteristics have been agreed to, or were suggested by Lieut. Colonel W. F. Lee (Inf.), Major I. M. Oseth (Inf.) and Major F. P. Tompkins (Cav.) during their visit to this depot on July 1, 1940.

3. The Infantry and Cavalry representatives expressed a desire that at least eight (8) of the trucks to be purchased be of the four (4) wheel steer type. Accordingly, the specification includes the applicable requirements in Paragraphs D-14. b. and D-22. a., paragraphs that should be mentioned in the Invitation for Bids as applying in the case of four (4) wheel steer trucks. In addition, the Invitation for Bids should stipulate that the two (2) wheel steer and four (4) wheel steer trucks shall be all of one make.

4. It is recommended that one (1) vehicle be included for continued test by this depot.

H. J. LAWES,
Lieut. Colonel, Quartermaster Corps,
Commanding.

Incl. - Spec. ES - No. 475
in trip.

13

\- 5 -

On July 3, 1940, officials at Holabird notified QMC HQ about the completion of specification ES-475. Note the reference to Colonel Oseth in item #2. He actively participated in the document's development. Cavalry also contributed. Lastly, team member Harold Crist of American Bantam (see page 56) also assisted the QM in its creation. HQ would quickly approve the depot's staff work.

Source: United States National Archives, College Park, Maryland

Adjutant General Authorizes Procurement

IMMEDIATE ACTION

SUBJECT: Light Vehicle Development.

AG 451
(6-15-40) M-D 4th Ind. SGS/hal

War Dept., July 5, 1940 - To the Chief of Ordnance and The Quartermaster General, IN TURN.

1. Attention is invited to the attached subcommittee report of the Ordnance Technical Committee, dated June 22, 1940, subject: Light Infantry and Cavalry Vehicles - Development of. The Military Characteristics of a Light Reconnaissance and Command Car, as recommended in paragraph 2 e of this report, are approved. The Quartermaster General is charged with the development and procurement of this vehicle.

2. As recommended in paragraph 3 b of the attached subcommittee report, it is desired that the Quartermaster General immediately initiate development and procurement of seventy (70) Light Reconnaissance and Command Cars in accordance with the approved military characteristics. The expenditure of not to exceed $175,000 from funds allotted the Quartermaster General is authorized for this purpose. When procured, these vehicles will be given an extended service test by the Infantry, Field Artillery and Cavalry; the number of vehicles to be supplied each of these arms for test to be in accordance with the recommendations contained in paragraph 3b of the attached report. If possible, it is desired that these vehicles be procured in time to be employed in the maneuvers scheduled to be held late this summer.

3. These vehicles will be tested under the supervision of the Infantry, Field Artillery and Cavalry Boards. The recommendations of these Boards will be coordinated by the Quartermaster Technical Committee, after which final recommendations will be submitted to this office by the Quartermaster General. In the conduct of this test, it is desired that consideration be given to the use of this vehicle in place of the motorcycle with side car and the tricycle type of vehicle.

By order of the Secretary of War:

/s/ A. P. Sullivan
Adjutant General.

3 Incls. n/c

99

APPENDIX "B"

89

The Adjutant General authorized the procurement to continue on July 5, 1940, and officially approved the $175,000 that the Chief of Staff had allocated for the effort.

Source: United States National Archives, College Park, Maryland

Payne's July 9, 1940, Letter

AMERICAN BANTAM CAR CO.
BUTLER, PA.

July 9, 1940

Colonel J. H. Johnson
Office of the Quartermaster General,
Washington, D. C.

Dear Sir:

This is to advise you that we are willing to undertake the delivery of seventy Bantam Cars, Four-Wheel Drive, 85 cubic inch motors, etc., as per specifications laid down by your department, at a price of $2500.00 per car, making a total contract in the amount of $175,000.00. If no further changes are made in the car, and providing order is given immediately, we can meet the delivery date of between August 20th and 30th. Some of the cars will probably be down before this time, however.

This price is f.o.b. Butler, Pa., and it will be necessary for the Government to either furnish drivers or trucks or some facility to assist in the delivery to the various maneuver centers which we are not familiar with at this time.

You may rest assured that we will cooperate one hundred percent with your department on any minor changes and would greatly appreciate it if you could arrange to have inspectors at our plant for facilitating the delivery of these first seventy cars.

Mr. Brown of your department has the detailed letter from our factory covering the above.

Yours very truly,

AMERICAN BANTAM CAR COMPANY

By Charles H. Payne

Charles H. Panye,
Assistant to the President

9

Anticipating a negotiated contract, Charles Payne wrote the QM General and offered to build the seventy vehicles at a cost of $2,500.00 per car. In a few short days, the Quartermaster would have a huge surprise for Bantam on how the procurement would continue.

Source: United States National Archives, College Park, Maryland

Battle of Britain Begins

On July 10, 1940, the Battle of Britain began. England would fight for its survival while the U.S. Army worked to build a light vehicle suitable for modern warfare.

Source: Public Domain

QMG Authorizes Bidding Process

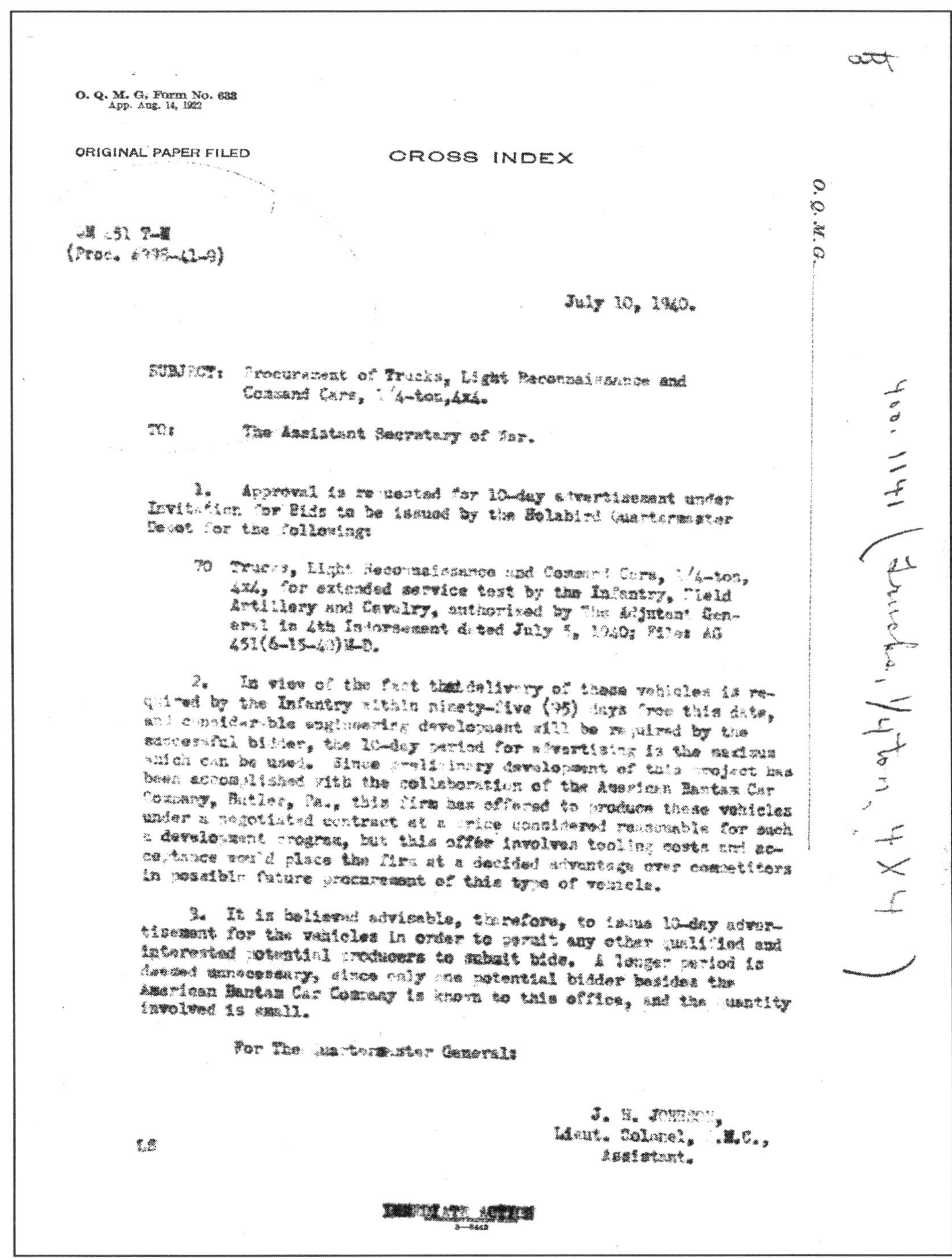

O. Q. M. G. Form No. 638
App. Aug. 14, 1922

ORIGINAL PAPER FILED

CROSS INDEX

O.Q.M.G.

QM 451 T-M
(Proc. #[illegible]-41-9)

July 10, 1940.

SUBJECT: Procurement of Trucks, Light Reconnaissance and Command Cars, 1/4-ton, 4x4.

TO: The Assistant Secretary of War.

1. Approval is requested for 10-day advertisement under Invitation for Bids to be issued by the Holabird Quartermaster Depot for the following:

70 Trucks, Light Reconnaissance and Command Cars, 1/4-ton, 4x4, for extended service test by the Infantry, Field Artillery and Cavalry, authorized by The Adjutant General in 4th Indorsement dated July 5, 1940; Files AG 451(6-15-40)M-D.

2. In view of the fact that delivery of these vehicles is required by the Infantry within ninety-five (95) days from this date, and considerable engineering development will be required by the successful bidder, the 10-day period for advertising is the maximum which can be used. Since preliminary development of this project has been accomplished with the collaboration of the American Bantam Car Company, Butler, Pa., this firm has offered to produce these vehicles under a negotiated contract at a price considered reasonable for such a development program, but this offer involves tooling costs and acceptance would place the firm at a decided advantage over competitors in possible future procurement of this type of vehicle.

3. It is believed advisable, therefore, to issue 10-day advertisement for the vehicles in order to permit any other qualified and interested potential producers to submit bids. A longer period is deemed unnecessary, since only one potential bidder besides the American Bantam Car Company is known to this office, and the quantity involved is small.

For The Quartermaster General:

J. H. JOHNSON,
Lieut. Colonel, Q.M.C.,
Assistant.

LS

IMMEDIATE ACTION

400.1141 (Trucks, 1/4 ton, 4x4)

On July 10, 1940, in a stunning move and harsh blow to Bantam, the QMG authorized a ten-day invitation to bid "in order to permit any other qualified and interested potential producers to submit bids". The QMG did note, "only one potential bidder besides the American Bantam Car Company is known to this effort".

Source: United States National Archives, College Park, Maryland

Holabird Notifed of Bid Process

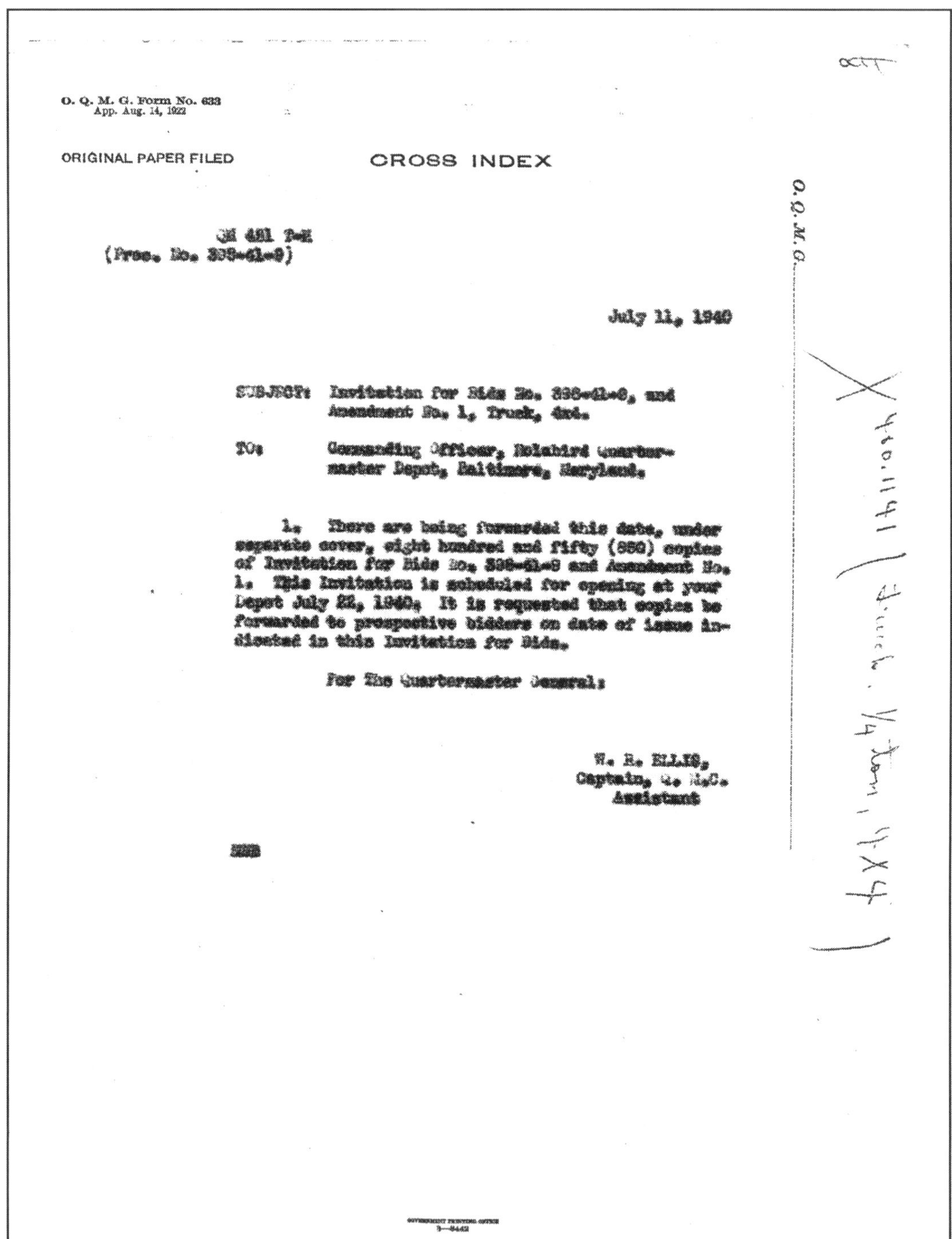

O. Q. M. G. Form No. 633
App. Aug. 14, 1922

ORIGINAL PAPER FILED

CROSS INDEX

O.Q.M.G.

QM 451 T-E
(Proc. No. 398-41-9)

July 11, 1940

SUBJECT: Invitation for Bids No. 398-41-9, and Amendment No. 1, Truck, 4x4.

TO: Commanding Officer, Holabird Quartermaster Depot, Baltimore, Maryland.

1. There are being forwarded this date, under separate cover, eight hundred and fifty (850) copies of Invitation for Bids No. 398-41-9 and Amendment No. 1. This Invitation is scheduled for opening at your Depot July 22, 1940. It is requested that copies be forwarded to prospective bidders on date of issue indicated in this Invitation for Bids.

For The Quartermaster General:

W. R. ELLIS,
Captain, Q. M.C.
Assistant

470.1141 / Truck, 1/4 ton, 4x4

The QMG notified Holabird of the bidding effort on July 11, 1940 and forwarded 850 copies of the bid documents for distribution by depot staff to prospective bidders.

Source: United States National Archives, College Park, Maryland

Invitation for Bids Sent Out

HOLABIRD QUARTERMASTER DEPOT
BALTIMORE, MARYLAND

July 11, 1940.

AMENDMENT NO. 1.

SUBJECT: Invitation for Bids No. 398-41-9,
Trucks, Light Reconn. & Command Car, 4x4.
Dated: July 11, 1940.
Opens: July 22, 1940.

TO: ALL BIDDERS.

Invitation for Bids No. 398-41-9, scheduled for opening at this Depot at 10:00 A.M. (Eastern Standard Time), on July 22, 1940, is amended and modified as follows:

SCHEDULE - Sheet No. 1.a. - ADD:

EXTRA NET COST for furnishing with each vehicle one (1) SPARE WHEEL, TIRE & TUBE (Par. D-18.c.). each ____________

Quartermaster Corps Tentative Specification ES-No. 475, dated July 2, 1940, is changed as follows:

Par. D-1.a. - DELETE: "twelve hundred and seventy-five (1275)" and substitute therefor: "thirteen hundred (1300)".

DELETE: "six hundred and twenty-five (625)" and substitute therefor: "six hundred (600)".

Par. D-18. - ADD:

"c. When specified in the Invitation for Bids, one (1) spare wheel, tire and tube shall be provided and mounted as required by Q.M. Drawing 08370-Z".

In all other respects the terms and conditions of the original Invitation for Bids will remain in force and effect.

This Amendment must be attached to Invitation for Bids No. 398-41-9 and must be made a part thereof when bid is submitted. If your original bid has already been mailed, this Amendment must be submitted (in triplicate), as a supplement thereto.

J. VAN NESS INGRAM,
Major, Q. M. Corps,
Purchasing & Contracting Officer.

____
(Name of Company)

____
(Signature of Official) (Title)

40/879

On July 11, 1940, the staff at Holabird sent the bid documentation to 135 firms with a deadline of July 22, 1940, to submit a proposal.

Source: United States National Archives, College Park, Maryland

Karl Probst

The decision to use a bid process caught the bankrupt Bantam Company completely by surprise. With no engineering staff to work on the bid, the Butler, PA company brought in veteran designer Karl Probst from Detroit to work with Harold Crist to complete the bid documentation.

Source: Photo Courtesy of Robert Brandon, Butler, PA

Probst Completes Design

Probst would not arrive in Butler until July 18th. Fenn introduced Probst to Crist and Crist quickly brought the Detroit engineer up-to-speed. He would begin his work that day. With only a break to see a Heddy Lamar movie and to catch some sleep, he completed his work by the end of the next day.

Source: Public Domain

Bantam's Bid Proposal Completed

Standard Form No. 31
Approved by the President
June 10, 1927

Invitation for Bids No. 398-41-9 Sheet No. 1a.

STANDARD GOVERNMENT FORM OF BID

(SUPPLY CONTRACT)

ORIGINAL
DUPLICATE
TRIPLICATE } Indicate which by erasure

Opening Date for this Bid

10:00 A. M., E.S.T., July 22, 1940.

To Purchasing & Contracting Officer,
Holabird Quartermaster Depot,
Baltimore, Maryland.

PLACE BUTLER, PENNSYLVANIA

DATE JULY 20, 1940

In compliance with your invitation for bids to furnish materials and supplies listed on the reverse hereof or on the accompanying schedules, numbered: Sheet No. 1b., and Q.M.C. Tentative Specification, ES-No. 475, dated July 2, 1940, the undersigned, AMERICAN BANTAM CAR COMPANY

a corporation organized and existing under the laws of the State of PENNSYLVANIA
a partnership consisting of
an individual trading as

of the city of BUTLER, PENNSYLVANIA
hereby proposes to furnish, within the time specified, the materials and supplies at the prices stated opposite the respective items listed on the schedules and agrees upon receipt of written notice of the acceptance of this bid within AT ONCE days (60 days if no shorter period be specified) after the date of opening of the bids, to execute, if required, the Standard Government Form of Contract (Standard Form No. 32) in accordance with the bid as accepted, and to give bond, if required, with good and sufficient surety or sureties, for the faithful performance of the contract, within 10 days after the prescribed forms are presented for signature.

Discount will be allowed for prompt payment as follows: 10 calendar days 1% percent; 20 calendar days .... percent; 30 calendar days .... percent; or as stated in the schedules.

(Time will be computed from date of the delivery of the supplies to carrier when final inspection and acceptance are at point of origin, or from date of delivery at destination or port of embarkation when final inspection and acceptance are at those points, or from date correct bill or voucher properly certified by the contractor is received if the latter date is later than the date of delivery.)

Ada Botte
(Witness to signature)

F H Fenn
(Full name of bidder) PRESIDENT

AMERICAN BANTAM CAR COMPANY

BUTLER, PENNSYLVANIA
(Address)

NOTE.—See Standard Government Instructions to Bidders and copy of the Standard Government Form of Contract, Bid Bond, and Performance Bond, which may be obtained upon application.

To insure prompt payment bills should be certified as follows: "I certify that the above bill is correct and just and that payment therefor has not been received."

10—1803 U. S. GOVERNMENT PRINTING OFFICE (OVER)

40/869

Bantam completed their bid proposal on July 20. The Bantam team would head to Baltimore to meet with Payne that same day.

Source: United States National Archives, College Park, Maryland

Baltimore, July 21, 1940

ES - No. 475.

F. QUESTIONNAIRE.

Bids will not receive consideration unless the bidder has furnished with his bid the accompanying Questionnaire, fully completed.

F-1. Truck. - Make BANTAM; model 40. Overall length 126" inches. Overall width 54" inches. Overall height, with body top raised, truck unloaded 71.5" inches. Shipping weight: 2-wheel steer trucks 1273; 4-wheel steer trucks 1323 lbs.; including all equipment, tools, tire chains, lubricants, and dunnage (less only fuel, water and the payload), i. e. everything that must be shipped. Weight of dunnage included in the shipping weight quoted above 85 lbs.

F-1a. Quantity of trucks that can be loaded in a freight car.

	Item No.	Quantity	Size and description of freight car
	1	8	50' AUTO BOX CAR
	2	8	50' AUTO BOX CAR
(NOTE)	3	6 to 8	PER TRUCK BY OUR OWN TRANSPORT TRUCKS

F-1b. Weight of truck completely equipped and including fuel, lubricants, water, tools and tire chains (less only the payload): 2-wheel steer trucks 1300; 4-wheel steer trucks 1350 lbs.

	Trucks 2-Wheel Steer	Trucks 4-wheel steer	
Gross weight allowance	1900	1950	lbs.
*Gross weight distribution:			
On front tires	665	675	lbs.
On rear tires	1235	1275	lbs.
*Payload allowance	600	600	lbs.

(*based on 1900 lbs. gross weight).

F-1c. Wheelbase 79" inches.

With truck fully equipped and loaded: Ground clearances under the following units will be: Front axle 8.5" inches; rear axle 8.5" inches; transmission 11.25" inches; transfer case skid shoe 9.5" inches; gas tank 21" inches; battery 21" inches; propeller shaft brake 9.5" inches. Angle of approach 45° degrees, departure 36° degrees.

Will the overall height of the truck comply with the requirements of Q. M. Drawing 08370-Z. YES.

Will the requirements of paragraph D-1. b. herein, concerning driver's vision ahead of the front of the truck, be fully complied with YES.

F-2. Frame. - Will the frame be of such a design and construction that it will support adequately the maximum gross loads imposed under the most severe operating conditions YES; Will the frame rear end be suitably braced for pintle mounting YES.

FEDERAL TRADE COMMISSION
DOCKET NO. 4959 COMMISSION'S EXHIBIT NO. 109 D
IN THE MATTER OF Willys Overland
DATE 7/15/44 WITNESS
HOWARD B SMITH, Official Reporter; By Hoyer

- 12 -

HOWARD B SMITH, Official Reporter; By Hoyer

At a long-past midnight meeting, Payne exploded when he saw the weight entered at 1,850 lbs.—well over the 1300 lbs. specification. He scrambled to have the bid forms retyped with a weight stated as 1,273 lbs. and completed them just in time to arrive at the 8:30 AM meeting later that day. The weight requirement would haunt the Jeep procurement's manufacturers.

Source: United States National Archives, College Park, Maryland

Camp Holabird, July 22, 1940

Only four manufacturers attended the bid meeting on July 22, 1940. Ford and Crosley failed to submit a proposal while Willys-Overland Motors, Inc. (the "other potential bidder" mentioned in the July 10th memo) offered a hand-written document. After some high drama about the 49-day delivery deadline, the award went to Bantam.

Source: Public Domain

CHAPTER 7

Building The First Jeep

The First Jeep - September 21, 1940. Source: Photo Courtesy of Robert Brandon, Butler, PA

Bids Technical Analysis

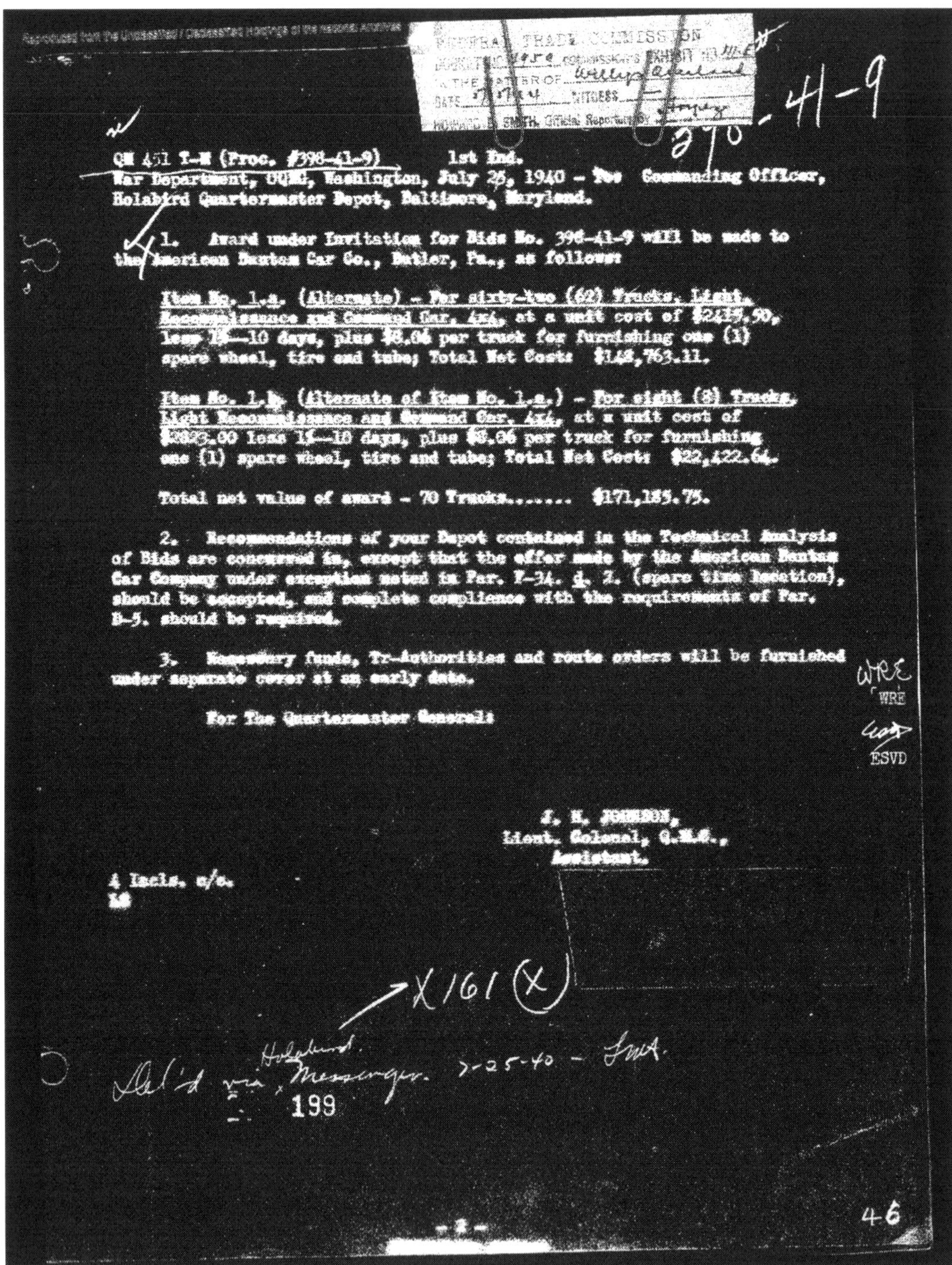

QM 451 T-M (Proc. #398-41-9) 1st Ind.
War Department, OQMG, Washington, July 25, 1940 - To Commanding Officer, Holabird Quartermaster Depot, Baltimore, Maryland.

1. Award under Invitation for Bids No. 398-41-9 will be made to the American Bantam Car Co., Butler, Pa., as follows:

Item No. 1.a. (Alternate) - For sixty-two (62) Trucks, Light, Reconnaissance and Command Car, 4x4, at a unit cost of $2415.50, less 1%—10 days, plus $8.06 per truck for furnishing one (1) spare wheel, tire and tube; Total Net Cost: $148,763.11.

Item No. 1.b. (Alternate of Item No. 1.a.) - For eight (8) Trucks, Light Reconnaissance and Command Car, 4x4, at a unit cost of $2823.00 less 1%—10 days, plus $8.06 per truck for furnishing one (1) spare wheel, tire and tube; Total Net Cost: $22,422.64.

Total net value of award - 70 Trucks....... $171,185.75.

2. Recommendations of your Depot contained in the Technical Analysis of Bids are concurred in, except that the offer made by the American Bantam Car Company under exception noted in Par. F-34. d. 2. (spare tire location), should be accepted, and complete compliance with the requirements of Par. B-5. should be required.

3. Necessary funds, Tr-Authorities and route orders will be furnished under separate cover at an early date.

For The Quartermaster General:

J. H. [illegible],
Lieut. Colonel, Q.M.C.,
Assistant.

4 Incls. n/c.

- 2 -

The Quartermaster conducted a thorough technical analysis of the submitted bids. The award would officially go to Bantam on July 25, 1940, with a number of stipulations that would become part of the contract.

Source: United States National Archives, College Park, Maryland

Contract Award Gives Them 49 Days

HEADQUARTERS
HOLABIRD QUARTERMASTER DEPOT
BALTIMORE, MARYLAND.

REGISTERED MAIL
RETURN RECEIPT
REQUESTED.

(Proc. Div.) August 1, 1940.

SUBJECT: Contract No. W-398-qm-8269 (O.I. #137) (Invitation for Bids No. 398-41-9)
American Bantam Car Co.,
Butler, Pa.
Gentlemen:

Confirming telegram dated July 25, 1940, you are hereby notified that award has been made to you under Invitation for Bids No. 398-41-9, as follows:

ITEM NO. 1.a: - 62 Each TRUCKS, MOTOR, GASOLINE, LIGHT RECONNAISSANCE and COMMAND CAR (FOUR WHEELS-FOUR WHEEL DRIVE), in accordance with Q.M.C. Tentative Specification ES-No. 475, dated July 2, 1940. To be equipped with FULL-FLOATING TYPE REAR AXLE:

Unit Cost	$2,415.50
Gross Cost of Item 1.a	$149,761.00
Less discount of 1% for payment in 10 days	1,497.61
Net Cost	$148,263.39
Plus $8.06 net per truck for one (1) spare wheel tire & tube	499.72
TOTAL NET COST OF Item 1.a	$148,763.11

ITEM NO. 1.b: - 8 Each TRUCKS, MOTOR, GASOLINE, LIGHT RECONNAISSANCE and COMMAND CAR (FOUR WHEELS - FOUR WHEEL DRIVE), in accordance with Q.M.C. Tentative Specification ES-No. 475, dated July 2, 1940. To be equipped with FULL-FLOATING TYPE REAR AXLE and FOUR WHEEL STEERING MECHANISM:

Unit Cost	$2,823.00
Gross Cost of Item 1.b.	22,584.00
Less discount of 1% for payment in 10 days	225.84
Net Cost	22,358.16
Plus $8.06 net per truck for one (1) spare wheel tire & tube	64.48
TOTAL NET COST OF Item 1.b.	$22,422.64
TOTAL GROSS COST	$173.070.56
TOTAL NET COST	$171,185.75

Prices quoted are F.O.B. your plant at Ardmore, Pennsylvania, for shipment on Government Bill of Lading or Driveaway by Government personnel.

The Army and Bantam completed a contract on August 1st, but final approval took until August 5th. Besides the weight, the other requirement that challenged the bidders revolved around what many considered impossible—the Army insisted on a prototype completed within 49 days. Bantam had until September 23, 1940, to build and deliver the revolutionary new vehicle.

Source: United States National Archives, College Park, Maryland

Battle of Britain Rages On

The Battle of Britain would continue throughout the forty-nine days Bantam had to build the prototype. While England continued to fight, unbeknownst to all, the fate of one of the great weapons of the war now rested in the hands of a bankrupt car company in Butler, PA.

Source: Public Domain

Harold Crist

A skilled draftsman and mechanical genius, Harold Crist, the former Stutz employee (first mentioned on page 56), played a significant role in the Jeep's development. To meet the impossible 49-day deadline, he had to utilize all the skills he had acquired during his decades-long career. He led the team that built the first Jeep.

A later model Stutz. Source: Public Domain - Bernard Spragg

Ralph Turner, Sr.

Crist brought on two other brilliant mechanics to form the core of the build-team. One of them, Ralph Turner, like Crist, possessed exceptional mechanical ability. He had worked as a watch repairman before Crist recruited him to join Bantam as its general foreman of the production line.

Main: Turner (hat) L. Inset: Turner L, Crist R. Source: Photos Courtesy of Robert Brandon, Butler, PA

Chester Hempfling

The third core member of Crist's build-team, Chester Hempfling began work in the automotive field with American Austin starting in 1930. He stayed on with Bantam and possessed a "jack-of-all-trades" skill set that complemented Probst, Crist, and Turner. In the picture above, taken later in his life, he holds the tin snips he used to cut the rounded hood on the prototype.

Source: Photo Courtesy of Robert Brandon, Butler, PA

The Chassis Rail

The team built the chassis rail first and would create the rest of the vehicle from there.

Source: Photo Courtesy of Robert Brandon, Butler, PA

Body Tube and Railing

They completed the body tube and rail assembly by September 4, 1940. Note the use of a calendar on the part to mark the date of its completion.

Source: Photo Courtesy of Robert Brandon, Butler, PA

Chassis Coming Together

By September 5th the chassis was built and engine mounted.

Source: Photo Courtesy of Robert Brandon, Butler, PA

Chassis and Drive Train

The chassis and drive train under construction.

Source: Photo Courtesy of Robert Brandon, Butler, PA

The Transmission and Transfer Case

The transmission and transfer case under construction.

Source: Photo Courtesy of Robert Brandon, Butler, PA

Chassis Assembly

The chassis assembly on September 10, 1940.

Source: Photo Courtesy of Robert Brandon, Butler, PA

The Vehicle Nearing Completion

As the vehicle came together, the major obstacle became whether or not the front axle would arrive in time or at all. From the start the major risk, as mentioned on page 65, the axle was manufactured by Spicer. They delivered the part on September 15, 1940. The photo above, taken after that date, shows the tires mounted on the axles both front and rear.

Source: Photo Courtesy of Robert Brandon, Butler, PA

The First Jeep

The first Jeep, September 21, 1940. After completing the vehicle the team rolled it out of the factory. Someone shouted, "get a Kodak" and took the photo above. Harold Crist sits in the driver's seat, Ralph Turner directly behind Crist and Karl Probst leans against the spare tire to the far left. The team named the vehicle the Bantam Reconnaissance Car or BRC for short.

Source: Photo Courtesy of Robert Brandon, Butler, PA

Parts Drawings

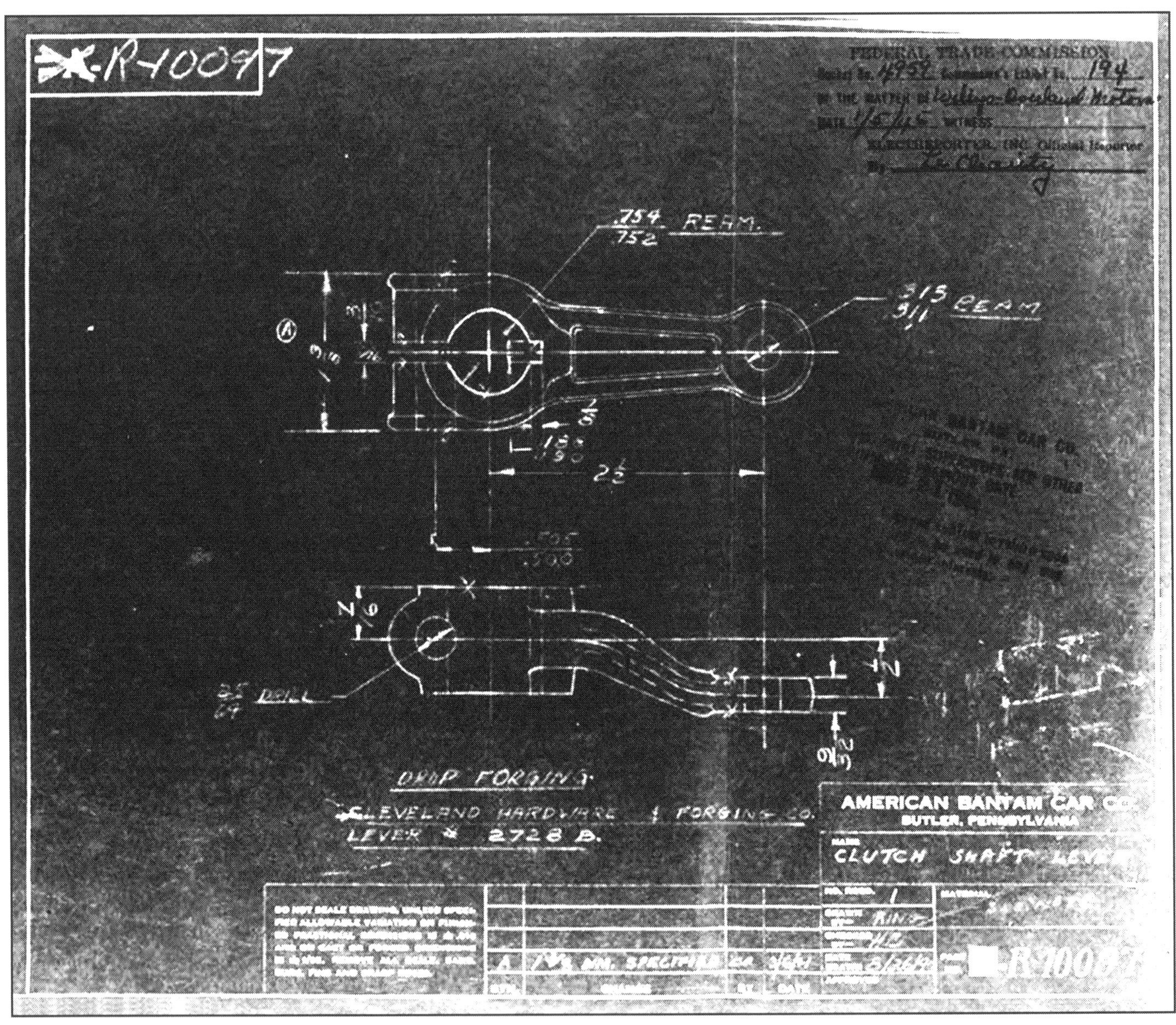

The team built many parts by hand and then made drawings after. Pictured above: the clutch shaft lever.

Source: United States National Archives, College Park Maryland

Parts List for the First 70 Bantams Ordered by the Army

AMERICAN BANTAM CAR COMPANY - BUTLER, PENNSYLVANIA Page 1. 184-A
1/2/45

FEDERAL TRADE COMMISSION
Docket No. 4957 Commission's Exhibit No. 184-A
IN THE MATTER OF Willys Overland Motors
DATE 1/4/45 WITNESS
ELECTREPORTER, INC. Official Reporter
By La Chanty

1/4-TON, 4x4 TRUCK ("JEEP"
FIRST 70
CONTRACT W-398-QM-8269

PART NO.	PART NAME	VENDOR	P.O. NO.	P.O. DATE	FIRST DATE	RECEIPTS QUANTITY
R-10259	Fuel Pump	A.C. Spark Plug Divn.	13617			
10044	Clutch Throwout Bearing	Aetna Ball Brg. Mfg. Co.	13516	8/23/40	9-9-40	70
10290	Rear View Mirror	American Automatic Device Co.	13528	8-27-40	8-23-40	1
10027	Accelerator Pedal	American Automatic Device Co.	13528	8-27-40	8-23-40	1
10402	Hand Brake Cable	American Cable Division	13593	Confirming 9-27-40	9-20-40	1
10123	Tire Chains	American Chain Division	13537	8-29-40	9-12-40	4 Pr.
(Various)	Sheet Metal Steel	American Rolling Mill Co.	13501-502	8-6-40	8-22, 8-27 & 9-3-40	75 Jobs
(Various)	Wiring	American Wire Division, Electric Auto-Lite Co.	(Wiring for Pilot Model made at Bantam and fitted on car by representative of American Wire Division, Electric Auto-Lite Co.)			
10048	Gas Tank	O. L. Anderson Co.	13521	8-23-40	9-4-40	2
---	Wheel & Rim Assemblies	Budd Wheel Company	13520	8-23-40	9-19-40	2 Sets
10111-171	Hubs & Drums	Budd Wheel Company	13522	8-23-40	9-19-40	2 Sets
	Hand Brake Assembly	Butler County Motor Co.	13535	8-28-40	8-28-40	1
10170	Gas Tank Strap Ends	Cleveland Hdw. & Forging Co.	13563	9-10-40	9-12-40	290
10097	Clutch Shaft Lever	Cleveland Hdw. & Forging Co.	13538	8-29-40	9-3-40	75
10100	Clutch Shaft Spring	Cleveland Wire Spring Co.	13552	9-4-40	9-8-40	107
10260	Lighting & Blackout Switch	Cole-Hersee Co.	13591	Confirming 9-27-40	9-16-40	2
10129-130	Tail Lamps-Service, Stop & Blackout	Corcoran-Brown Lamp Divn.	13583	Confirming 9-19-40	9-17-40	1 Pr.
	Blackout Head Lamps	Corcoran-Brown Lamp Divn.	13583	9-19-40	9-17-40	1 Pr.
10186	Steering Column Bracket	Correct Manufacturing Co.	13570	9-16-40	9-25-40	2
10187	Exhaust Outlet Elbow	Correct Manufacturing Co.	13570	9-16-40	9-25-40	2
10185	Carburetor Air Horn	Correct Manufacturing Co.	13567	9-13-40	9-25-40	2
	Head Lamps	R. E. Dietz Co.	13555	9-5-40	9-1-40	1 Pr.

Editor's note: BANTAM ADDED THIS NOTE AT THE END THIS 4-PAGE PARTS LIST.

In addition to this list of components, many small items were picked up at local automobile supply houses, numerous small parts were fabricated in our plant and some standard Bantam parts were used. Some sample parts were also used and standard nuts, bolts, washers, etc., were obtained from our inventory, or purchased locally.

Thousands of parts, both hand-built and off the shelf, went into the BRC.

Source: United States National Archives, College Park, Maryland.

Delivery of the BRC

The final act of the forty-nine day drama involved delivering the prototype to Holabird on time to avoid financial penalties. On September 23, 1940—after only one day of testing—the team drove the vehicle from Butler in the Pittsburgh area of western Pennsylvania onto the grounds of the depot in the Baltimore, Maryland area. They arrived with only a half-hour to spare.

Source: Library of Congress. Public Domain

CHAPTER 8

Testing and Accepting the BRC

The BRC Undergoing Testing at Holabird. Source: John W. Underwood, Heritage Press, 1965

BRC at Holabird

The BRC would undergo rigorous testing and trials over the four weeks following its delivery. The Army's goal: break this vehicle in any way possible.

Source: Public Domain

Troops Trying out the BRC

Troops getting used to the BRC.

Source: United States National Archives, College Park, Maryland

An Easy Test

Troops testing the BRC on a mild slope.

Source: Public Domain

Seeing What the BRC Can Do

Holabird testers raised the bar and began to push the BRC to see how well it could perform.

Source: Public Domain

The BRC in the Mud

A little mud would not stop the BRC!

Source: John W. Underwood, Heritage Press, 1965

How Deep is that Mud!

Here the test driver leans over to see how deep the left rear tire had sunk. The BRC's four-wheel drive would make it seem not deep at all! During one outing, a Cavalry general lifted the rear end of the prototype BRC by himself. From the results of that "test", he concluded that the "officially" overweight vehicle met the weight "requirement". Thus he settled the BRC weight issue once and for all.

Source: John W. Underwood, Heritage Press, 1965

Cross-Country Ability

A key requirement for the new vehicle from the beginning centered around cross-country ability. This photo shows the BRC moving quickly over a rough road demonstrating that ability.

Source: John W. Underwood, Heritage Press, 1965

Test Reports

October 28, 1940

SUBJECT: Final Inspection Report on Pilot Model 1/4-Ton, 4 x 4 (Bantam) Chassis - Light Reconnaissance and Command Car. (Contract No. W-398-qm-8269). (Pilot Truck, Item 1. a.) (Invitation for Bids No. 398-41-9)

TO: The Purchasing and Contracting Officer, Holabird Quartermaster Depot, Baltimore, Maryland.

1. The following comments covering body, cowl, windshield, hood, front fenders, headlights, gas tank and brush guard are furnished in addition to the Inspection Report on Pilot Model 1/4-Ton, 4 x 4 (Bantam) Chassis, Light Reconnaissance and Command Car, submitted under date of October 23, 1940:

PAR. D-25. a. The brush guard must be of stronger construction and shall include the headlight guards required by Drawing 08570-Z.

The original front fender equipment was not suitable and will be replaced by fenders of a design stipulated below.

The hood catch would not remain latched when the car was resting on uneven terrain. A suitable catch shall be provided at the front and safety catches must be mounted on each side of the hood.

Louvres must be inserted in the hood sides on production trucks.

The design of the windshield is not satisfactory. The manufacturer shall furnish a windshield assembly of adequate strength and suitable design on the production trucks.

The windshield wiper was placed too near to the left side of the windshield. Stops must be provided to prevent the blade being rotated off the windshield.

The headlight brackets cracked the fender skirt to which they were attached and the headlight lens clamp screws loosened from vibration, permitting the lens to become loose. The left front headlight interfered with opening and closing of the hood. Headlights properly placed and brackets of a suitable design must be provided.

The Holabird testers did all they could to break the BRC. While the new vehicle bent, it did not break. Holabird staff produced three test reports, the final one on October 28, 1940. While suggesting numerous improvements, overall the Army came away very favorably impressed with the BRC and executed the contract to build sixty-nine more.

Source: United States National Archives, College Park, Maryland

BRC Final Approval

QM 451 (398-41-9)
(Trucks, ¼-ton, 4x4)
Ltr. to TAG - Cont'd.

FEDERAL TRADE COMMISSION
DOCKET NO. 4959 COMMISSION'S EXHIBIT NO. 117B
IN THE MATTER OF Willys Overland
DATE 5/15/44 WITNESS
HOWARD B SMITH, Official Reporter; By Hoyer

b. The pilot model has been examined by the interested arms except the Armored Force and is being tested at the Holabird Quartermaster Depot. The Commanding Officer of the Depot has informally reported that the test is practically completed and the vehicle found satisfactory, subject to modifications found necessary as a result of the test.

3. a. The recommendations contained in the basic report are concurred in subject to availability of funds and to the following:

(1) Negotiations recommended in sub-paragraph (2) of recommendations in basic report should be based upon the prior approval and acceptance of a pilot model submitted for test.

(2) Negotiations should not be allowed to delay the production of the fifteen hundred (1,500) vehicles.

(3) Each manufacturer should be required to submit prices and deliveries on additional quantities on the basis of 2,500, 5,000, 7,500 and 10,000 vehicles, these prices and deliveries to be binding should it be found desirable to extend contract.

4. Based upon the latest information available to this office as to requirements of tactical and administrative vehicles, the balance of funds F.Y. 1941 remaining available for procurement of motor vehicles is estimated to be approximately $19,000,000. Present requirements do not include replacement centers, schools, administrative requirements that may develop from instructions contained in letter AG 451 (9-24-40)M-D-M, dated October 7, 1940, subject: Supply of Administrative Motor Vehicles, and Air Corps expansion requirements, including service units pertaining thereto not covered in Air Corps Units already designated for activation and motorization.

5. Included in the present requirements program are 11,818 motorcycles with side car, the estimated cost of which is $5,909,000. Procurement of these vehicles is not authorized pending development of a more suitable type. As one of the uses of the Light Command Reconnaissance Truck is considered to be as a replacement for the motorcycle with sidecar, funds required for this project, approximately $1,875,000.00, might properly be applied against this item, if approved.

6. Attached is a letter, inclosure No. 2, from the Willys-Overland Company dated October 18, 1940, received after preparation of the attached report, which changes the unit cost of the vehicle from $1,581.38 to $1,235.00.

-2-

3 (3)

Even before the test reports came in, the Army approved the vehicle on October 22, 1940. The Quartermaster General reported to the Adjutant General that, "the commanding officer of the Depot has informally reported that the test is practically completed and the vehicle found satisfactory."

Source: United States National Archives, College Park, Maryland

Battle of Britain Ends

The most significant phase of the Battle of Britain ended on October 31, 1940. By that time Hitler had postponed Germany's invasion of England. The island nation would fight on.

A Hawker Hurricane Fighter. Source: Public Domain - Adrian Pingstone

Willys-Overland Motors, Inc.

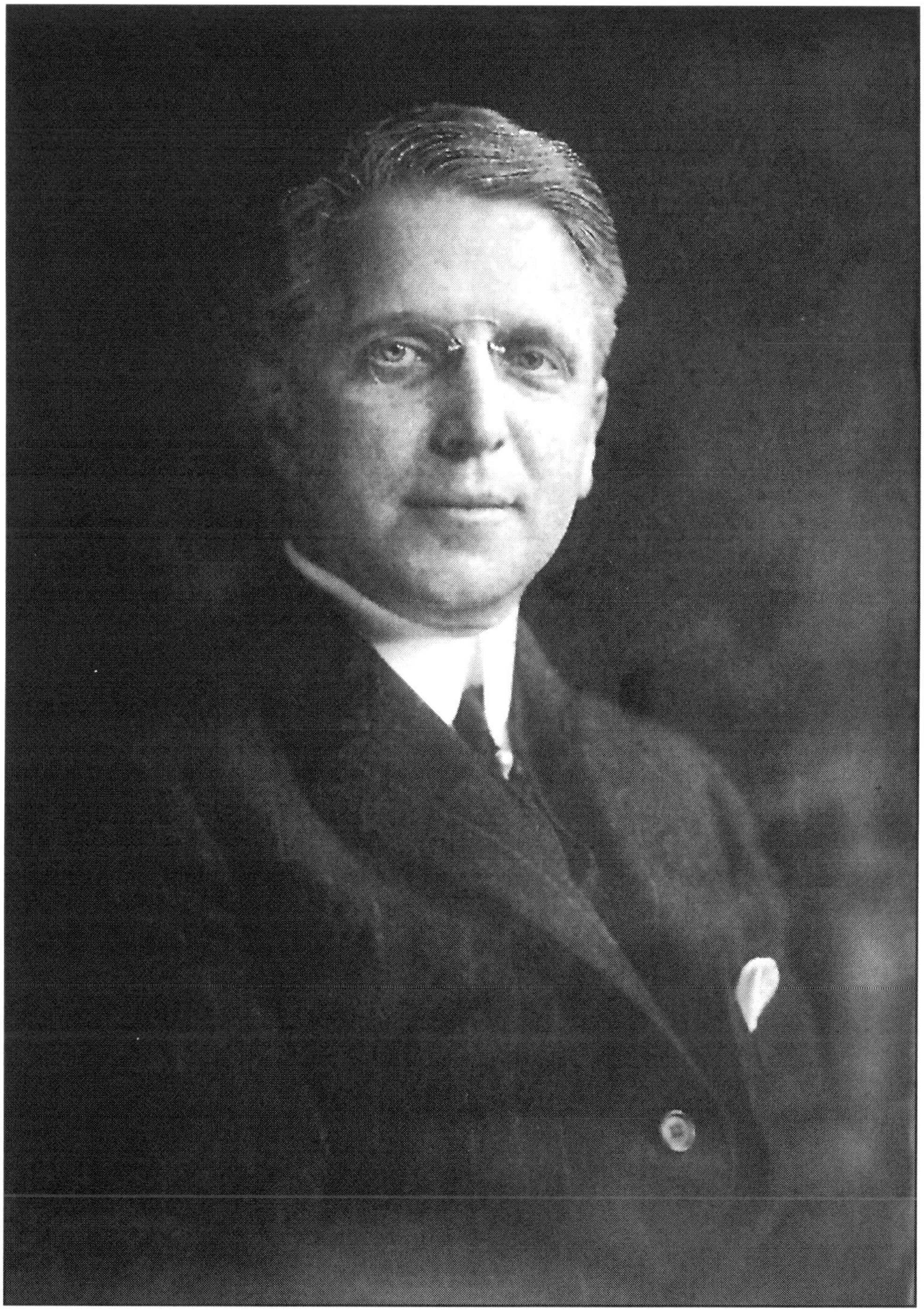

John North Willys c. 1917 - Founder of Willys-Overland Motors, Inc. Source: Public Domain

John North Willys

Born in upstate New York in 1873, John North Willys, like Roy Evans, demonstrated an entrepreneurial streak from a young age. He founded Willys-Overland in 1909 and headed this giant of the early automotive years until his death in 1935.

Source: Courtesy of the Patrick Foster Historical Collection

1904 Overland Model 15

A pioneer in the automotive industry, the Overland company of Terre Haute, Indiana, built excellent vehicles, but experienced financial problems throughout its short life. After working with the firm during most of the first decade of the 20th century, John Willys bought the firm in 1908 and renamed it Willys-Overland Motor Company in 1912.

Source: Courtesy of the Patrick Foster Historical Collection

Willys Moves Firm to Toledo, Ohio

Willys moved the company to Toledo during the 1910s. Despite being bought out after World War II, the firm would remain based there until the final demise of the Willys name in 1963.

Source: Public Domain

1914 Willys-Overland Model 79C

Three-Quarter View, Overland Model 79-C

Four-Passenger Coupe

Specifications and Equipment—Motor, 4⅛ x 4½ in. *35 horsepower. Wheelbase,* 114 in. *Ignition,* new model Splitdorf magneto and battery. *Rear Axle,* three-quarter floating; Hyatt bearings. *Tires,* 33 x 4 in., quick detachable. *Finish,* Overland green with light green striping, black hubs, nickel and aluminum trimmings. *Equipment,* seven electric lights; storage battery;

An excellent car for the 1910s, the Willys-Overland Model 79C shows the improvements in Willys vehicles since 1904.

Source: Courtesy of the Patrick Foster Historical Collection

1921 Willys-Overland Roadster

Willys continually improved their vehicles through the years. Despite financial difficulties in the early part of the decade, the firm would prosper during the "Roaring Twenties".

Source: Courtesy of the Patrick Foster Historical Collection

1927 Willys Whippet

WHIPPET LANDAU IN THE PAINTED DESERT—COLORFUL WONDERLAND OF ARIZONA

As the 1920s came to a close the very successful Willys-Overland Motor Company continued to build a variety of vehicles.

Source: Courtesy of the Patrick Foster Historical Collection

1937 Willys Sedan

Willys-Overland struggled during the Great Depression. The firm nearly went bankrupt, and John Willys died in 1935 with the company he founded on the ropes. However, the enterprise managed to ride out the storm and after John Willys' death, the firm's name changed to Willys-Overland Motors, Inc.

Source: Courtesy of the Patrick Foster Historical Collection

Ward M. Canady

Ward M. Canady became President of Willys-Overland Motors, Inc. in 1935. He would become Chairman of the Board in 1939 and would remain with the firm throughout the Jeep procurement.

Source: Courtesy of the Patrick Foster Historical Collection

Joseph Frazer

Joseph Frazer assumed the Presidency of Willys-Overland Motors, Inc. in 1939 when Ward Canady became Chairman. Similar to Frank Fenn, he would provide the executive leadership for Willys throughout the Jeep procurement.

Source: Courtesy of the Patrick Foster Historical Collection

Delmar Roos

Delmar Roos joined Willys-Overland Motors, Inc. as Vice-President of Engineering in 1938. He would provide the hands-on engineering and oversight to the building of all of Willys' Jeeps during 1940 and 1941.

Source: Courtesy of the Patrick Foster Historical Collection

Willys' Initial Meetings with the Army

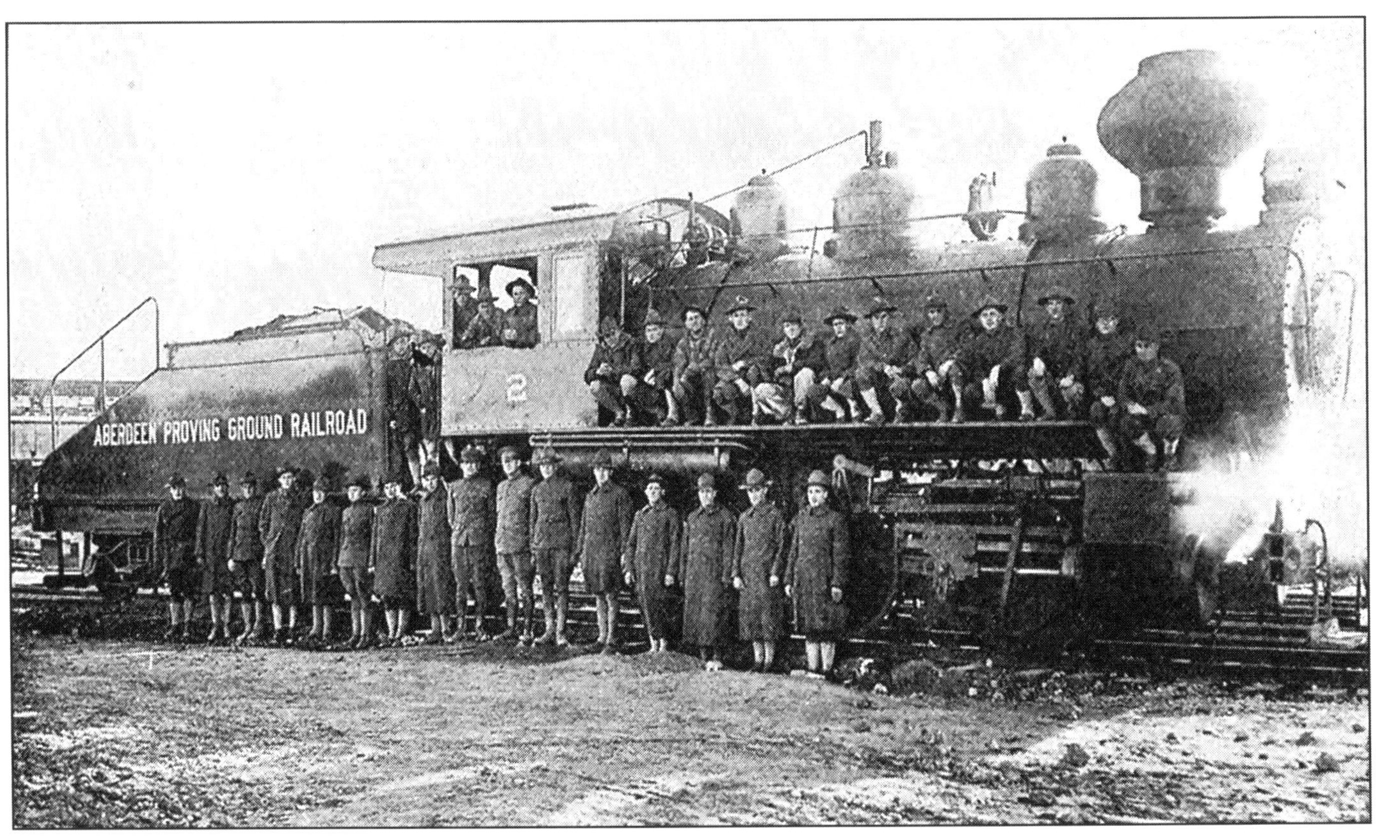

Willys officials held initial meetings with Army officials in the fall of 1939 at various locations, including the Aberdeen Proving Grounds, regarding a light reconnaissance vehicle. From these discussions the firm developed general ideas as to the military's needs.

Source: Public Domain

Willys Meets with Infantry Officers

Willys executives met with Infantry personnel in early 1940 including General Walter Short (pictured above) and Major Howie of Howie Weapons Carrier fame. Willys had "skin in the game" for the light vehicle, but would not participate in the car's development again until the July 1940 bid process.

Source: Public Domain

Willys Bids for the First Jeep

Invitation for Bids No. 398-41-3 Sheet No. 1a.

STANDARD GOVERNMENT FORM OF BID

(SUPPLY CONTRACT)

92-C

FEDERAL TRADE COMMISSION ORIGINAL
DOCKET NO. 4959 DUPLICATE
IN THE MATTER OF TRIPLICATE
DATE 4-18-44 WITNESS
EDWARD B. SMITH
Reporter

Opening Date for this Bid

10:00 A. M., E.S.T., July 22, 1940

To Purchasing & Contracting Officer, Holabird Quartermaster Depot, Baltimore, Maryland.

PLACE Toledo, Ohio

DATE July 20, 1940

In compliance with your invitation for bids to furnish materials and supplies listed on the reverse hereof or on the accompanying schedules, numbered: Sheet No. 1b., and Q.M.C. Tentative Specification ES-No. 475, dated July 2, 1940, the undersigned, Willys-Overland Motors, Inc.

a corporation organized and existing under the laws of the State of Delaware

a partnership consisting of

an individual trading as

of the city of Toledo, Ohio

hereby proposes to furnish, within the time specified, the materials and supplies at the prices stated opposite the respective items listed on the schedules and agrees upon receipt of written notice of the acceptance of this bid within 30 days (60 days if no shorter period be specified) after the date of opening of the bids, to execute, if required, the Standard Government Form of Contract (Standard Form No. 32) in accordance with the bid as accepted, and to give bond, if required, with good and sufficient surety or sureties, for the faithful performance of the contract, within 10 days after the prescribed forms are presented for signature.

No Discount will be allowed for prompt payment ~~as follows: 10 calendar days .... percent; 20~~ calendar days .... percent; 30 calendar days .... percent; or as stated in the schedules.

(Time will be computed from date of the delivery of the supplies to carrier when final inspection and acceptance are at point of origin, or from date of delivery at destination or port of embarkation when final inspection and acceptance are at those points, or from date correct bill or voucher properly certified by the contractor is received if the latter date is later than the date of delivery.)

(Witness to signature)

(Full name of bidder)

By

(Address)

Willys-Overland EXHIBIT 4 p. 3
OBTAINED 7/6/43 193
BY M R Purrington ATTORNEY-EXAMINER
FILE NO. 28-2-14096

NOTE.—See Standard Government Instructions to Bidders and copy of the Standard Government Form of Contract, Bid Bond, and Performance Bond, which may be obtained upon application.

To insure prompt payment bills should be certified as follows: "I certify that the above bill is correct and just and that payment therefor has not been received."

10—1803 O U.S. GOVERNMENT PRINTING OFFICE

(OVER)

40/869

Over

When a Request for Bids arrived at Willys in July 1940, it took them totally by surprise. Although they worked diligently to secure the work, the award went to Bantam.

Source: United States National Archives, College Park, Maryland

Willys Builds a Prototype at its Own Expense

Despite not securing the award to build the first Jeep, Willys worked out a deal with Quartermaster officials to build a prototype at their own expense. The Toledo firm would remain a player in the effort to build a light vehicle for the Army.

Delmar Roos with Willys Quad prototype. Source: Courtesy of the Patrick Foster Historical Collection

CHAPTER 10

Willys Builds Prototypes While Ford Emerges

Willys Prototype Jeep - The Willys Quad. Source: Public Domain

General Design and Layouts

The Willys build team completed their initial work by August 15, 1940. A critical decision for the Toledo group revolved around using their Go-Devil engine. While providing more horsepower than Bantam's engine, it also added to the vehicle's weight. Meeting the weight requirement would haunt Willys throughout the Jeep procurement.

Source: Courtesy of the Patrick Foster Historical Collection

Willys Builds a Prototype

Working diligently, the Willys group built their prototype during the summer and into the fall of 1940.

Source: Public Domain

The Willys Quad

Willys completed their prototype on November 4, 1940, and named it the Willys Quad. Ironically, Spicer provided the axles for Willys as they represented the only supplier that could manufacture that critical part.

Source: Public Domain

Willys Quad Parts List

R - 82-A

FEDERAL TRADE COMMISSION
DOCKET NO. 4959 RESPONDENTS EXHIBIT NO. 82-A
IN THE MATTER OF Willys-overland
DATE 8/7/44 WITNESS — Stone
ELECTREPORTER, INC., Official Reporter
By Moral

Name of Part Part No.	Purchase Order No.	Date Issued	Date Received
2 FRONT AXLES complete with Hubs, double anchor Bendix 9 x 1-3/4" Brakes, 16" Budd Wheels and Rims Spicer Mfg. Co. Toledo, Ohio.	37409	8/21/40	10/19/40 1st 10/26/40 2nd
2 REAR AXLES complete with Hubs, double anchor Bendix 9 x 1-3/4" Brakes, 16" Budd Wheels and Rims Spicer Mfg. Co. Toledo, Ohio	37409	8/21/40	10/19/40 1st 10/26/40 2nd
2 TRANSFER CASE complete with PROPELLER SHAFT, Brake and Drum (for mounting on 2 Warner Gear Company Transmission T-84 for overdrive) Spicer Mfg. Co. Toledo, Ohio	37409	8/21/40	10/19/40 1st 10/26/40 2nd
2 Pair - COMBINATION SEAL BEAM HEAD LAMPS with BLACKOUT PARKING LAMPS Part No. E-37756 Corcoran Brown Lamp Company Cincinnati, Ohio	37941	8/21/40	10/4/40
2 Pair - COMBINATION SERVICE, TAIL, STOP, LICENSE PLATE and BLACKOUT TAIL LAMPS Part No. E-37757 Corcoran Brown Lamp Company, Cincinnati, Ohio.	37941	8/21/40	10/4/40
2 Pair - COMBINATION BLACKOUT TAIL AND BLACKOUT STOP LAMPS Part No. E-37758 Corcoran Brown Lamp Company, Cincinnati, Ohio	37941	8/21/40	10/4/40
8 Pair - Red Reflectors Part No. E-37759 Corcoran Brown Lamp Company, Cincinnati, Ohio.	37941	8/21/40	10/4/40

Similar to Bantam, Willys used many parts in its prototype both custom-built and off-the-shelf.

Source: United States National Archives, College Park, Maryland

The Willys Quad Arrives at Holabird

AGREEMENT

DATE November 13, 1940.

For the purpose of ascertaining whether suitable for military use, request is hereby made to the War Department to examine and test One (1) each - 1/4 ton 4 x 4 - 2-wheel steer and one (1) 1/4 ton 4 x 4 4-wheel steer, Light Reconnaissance and Command Cars.

which will be delivered to Holabird Quartermaster Depot, Baltimore, Maryland. for that purpose and removed therefrom upon completion or conclusion of the test without any cost, responsibility, or obligation of any kind on the part of the Government except to furnish the undersigned a report, through the Office of The Quartermaster General, Washington, D. C., to show operating conditions of the test, failures, and defects noted in the equipment and whether or not as furnished it is suitable for Army use. It is understood and hereby agreed that neither said report nor any part thereof will be used for sales or for advertising purposes.

In the event that the results of the test of the initial test sample prove unsatisfactory for any reason and the undersigned desires to submit additional samples for test by the Government, it is understood and agreed that the undersigned will bear the cost of such additional test or tests.

Any failure, breakage, or other damage sustained during or as a result of this test will be promptly replaced or paid for by the undersigned. The test may be concluded at any time without any obligation on the part of the United States.

Delmar G. Roos Vice Pres

WILLYS OVERLAND MOTOR CAR COMPANY, INC.

39/1328

After some testing, the Willys Quad headed to Holabird on November 11, 1940, arriving on November 13, 1940.

Source: United States National Archives, College Park, Maryland

Ford Motor Company

Henry Ford founded the Ford Motor Company at the age of 39. His firm would grow into one of the giants of the automotive industry during the 20th century.

Source: Public Domain

1923 Ford Model T

The Ford Model T, which debuted in 1908, became one of the best-selling cars of the early 20th century before its discontinuation in 1927.

Source: Public Domain

1931 Ford Model A

Ford replaced the Model T with the Model A in 1928. The firm produced the Model A until 1932 and after that year made various models throughout the 1930s.

Source: Public Domain

The QMC Contacts Ford

The Quartermaster Corps. contacted Ford in early October 1940 in regard to building a prototype. After meeting on October 4, 1940, the Dearborn, Michigan manufacturer (located near Detroit, pictured above circa 1910) agreed to build a vehicle.

Source: Public Domain

Ford Builds a Prototype

Ford hand-built their prototype in the Ford development shop in Dearborn, Michigan (most likely near, or on the grounds of, the River Rouge plant pictured above) during October and November 1940. They named the vehicle the GP1, with the G standing for government and the P for a car with a wheelbase of 80 inches. They nicknamed it the Pygmy.

Source: Public Domain

Ford Pygmy Arrives at Holabird

Ford delivered the Pygmy to Holabird on November 23, 1940.

Source: United States Army Archives. Public Domain

CHAPTER 11

The Competition to Build 1,500 Jeeps Begins

Camp Holabird—focal point of Jeep work, fall-winter 1940. Source: Public Domain

Lieutenant General Edmund Gregory

Lieutenant General Edmund P. Gregory, the Quartermaster General, would play a pivotal role in the Jeep procurement during the fall and winter of 1940. Through events worthy of a Hollywood thriller, by spring 1941 the Army would have three vendors vying to build the Jeep for the military.

Source: Public Domain

Fenn's October 4th Quote

EXECUTIVE OFFICES
AMERICAN BANTAM CAR COMPANY
BUTLER, PA.
U.S.A.
October 4, 1940

Major J. Van Ness Ingram, U.S.A.
Camp Holabird
Baltimore, Maryland

FEDERAL TRADE COMMISSION
DOCKET NO. 4959 COMMISSION'S EXHIBIT NO. 112-a
IN THE MATTER OF Willys Overland
DATE 7/15/44 WITNESS
HOWARD B. SMITH, Official Reporter; By Hayes

Dear Sir:

Confirming Mr. Payne's conversation with you this afternoon, we are pleased to quote you the following figures:

(1) On an initial order for 500 cars, incorporating the body changes, etc., which have already been requested, we will furnish these cars for $1,173.00 each, which is a reduction of in excess of 50% under the first 70 cars. This figure includes $50 per car for machine tools, which will be the property of the U.S. Army in the plant of the Spicer Manufacturing Corporation at Toledo, Ohio, and will be so marked by the Army and removable by them at any time. It will be necessary to buy these machine tools, in order to fabricate small size 4-wheel drive equipment which goes into these cars.

(2) On the second lot of 500 cars, the price will be reduced to $938.00 each.

(3) On subsequent orders, totaling 3,000 units on a single release, the price will be in the immediate vicinity of $700.00. These prices apply to the regular 4 X 4, full-floating, two-wheel steer cars. On larger orders the price can be substantially reduced.

We shall be glad to have you incorporate in all contracts a clause to the effect that any savings effected over the above quotations will be refunded to the government after allowing us a 10% profit because the prices quoted herein are "pressure prices". In other words, we have not had an opportunity to completely shop the market on parts not made in our own factory because of the time element involved.

We assume that approval on the present pilot will be given about October 18. Under the terms of our present contract, we have 26 days from that date in which to produce the remaining 61 two-wheel steer jobs, which, based on October 18, will take until November 6, plus additional time, which we assume you will allow for changes which may be required. Beyond that time, we have another two weeks in which to fabricate the 8 4-wheel steer cars covered by our contract, which means it will probably be sometime between the first and 15th of December before the present order is completed, depending of course on the time necessary for changes.

With the above in mind, Major, we can, according to our present arrangements with Spicer, start delivery of cars on any future orders, if immediately released, during the first week of January, 1941; and we can complete an order for 500 cars comfortably within sixty days time.

Not really having a plan after the acceptance of the BRC, the QMC decided to order 500 vehicles from all three vendors. This would raise objections due to the fact Willys and Ford had not delivered, nor had the Army accepted, a prototype—a must to receive a contract. On October 4, 1940, Frank Fenn quoted the Army a price of $1,173.00 per vehicle for an initial order of 500 cars.

Source: United States National Archives, College Park, Maryland

Rice's October 8th Quote

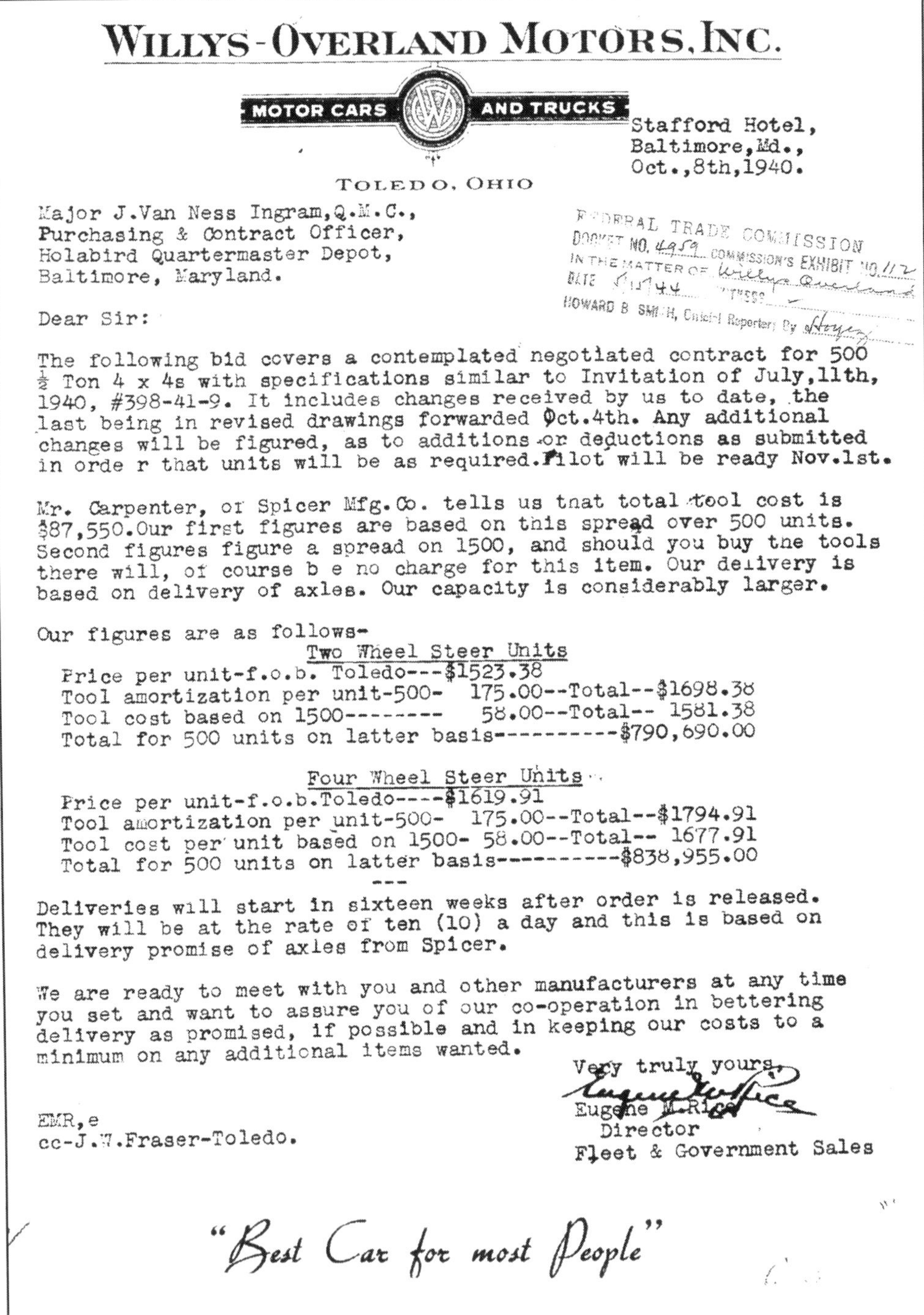

WILLYS-OVERLAND MOTORS, INC.

MOTOR CARS AND TRUCKS

TOLEDO, OHIO

Stafford Hotel,
Baltimore, Md.,
Oct., 8th, 1940.

Major J. Van Ness Ingram, Q.M.C.,
Purchasing & Contract Officer,
Holabird Quartermaster Depot,
Baltimore, Maryland.

FEDERAL TRADE COMMISSION
DOCKET NO. 4959 COMMISSION'S EXHIBIT NO. 112
IN THE MATTER OF Willys-Overland
DATE 5-1-44 WITNESS
HOWARD B. SMITH, Official Reporter; By

Dear Sir:

The following bid covers a contemplated negotiated contract for 500 ½ Ton 4 x 4s with specifications similar to Invitation of July, 11th, 1940, #398-41-9. It includes changes received by us to date, the last being in revised drawings forwarded Oct. 4th. Any additional changes will be figured, as to additions or deductions as submitted in orde r that units will be as required. Pilot will be ready Nov. 1st.

Mr. Carpenter, of Spicer Mfg. Co. tells us that total tool cost is $87,550. Our first figures are based on this spread over 500 units. Second figures figure a spread on 1500, and should you buy the tools there will, of course b e no charge for this item. Our delivery is based on delivery of axles. Our capacity is considerably larger.

Our figures are as follows-

Two Wheel Steer Units

Price per unit-f.o.b. Toledo---$1523.38
Tool amortization per unit-500- 175.00--Total--$1698.38
Tool cost based on 1500-------- 58.00--Total-- 1581.38
Total for 500 units on latter basis----------$790,690.00

Four Wheel Steer Units

Price per unit-f.o.b. Toledo----$1619.91
Tool amortization per unit-500- 175.00--Total--$1794.91
Tool cost per unit based on 1500- 58.00--Total-- 1677.91
Total for 500 units on latter basis----------$838,955.00

Deliveries will start in sixteen weeks after order is released. They will be at the rate of ten (10) a day and this is based on delivery promise of axles from Spicer.

We are ready to meet with you and other manufacturers at any time you set and want to assure you of our co-operation in bettering delivery as promised, if possible and in keeping our costs to a minimum on any additional items wanted.

Very truly yours,

Eugene M. Rice
Director
Fleet & Government Sales

EMR, e
cc-J.W. Fraser-Toledo.

"Best Car for most People"

Eugene Rice, Willys' government sales representative, responded to the request for quotes on October 8th, with a price of $1,581.38 per unit.

Source: United States National Archives, College Park, Maryland

Henry L. Stimson

The Secretary of War, Henry L. Stimson, along with Adjutant General Emory Adams, would make a number of critical decisions related to the Jeep procurement.

Source: Public Domain

Payne's October 14th Letter

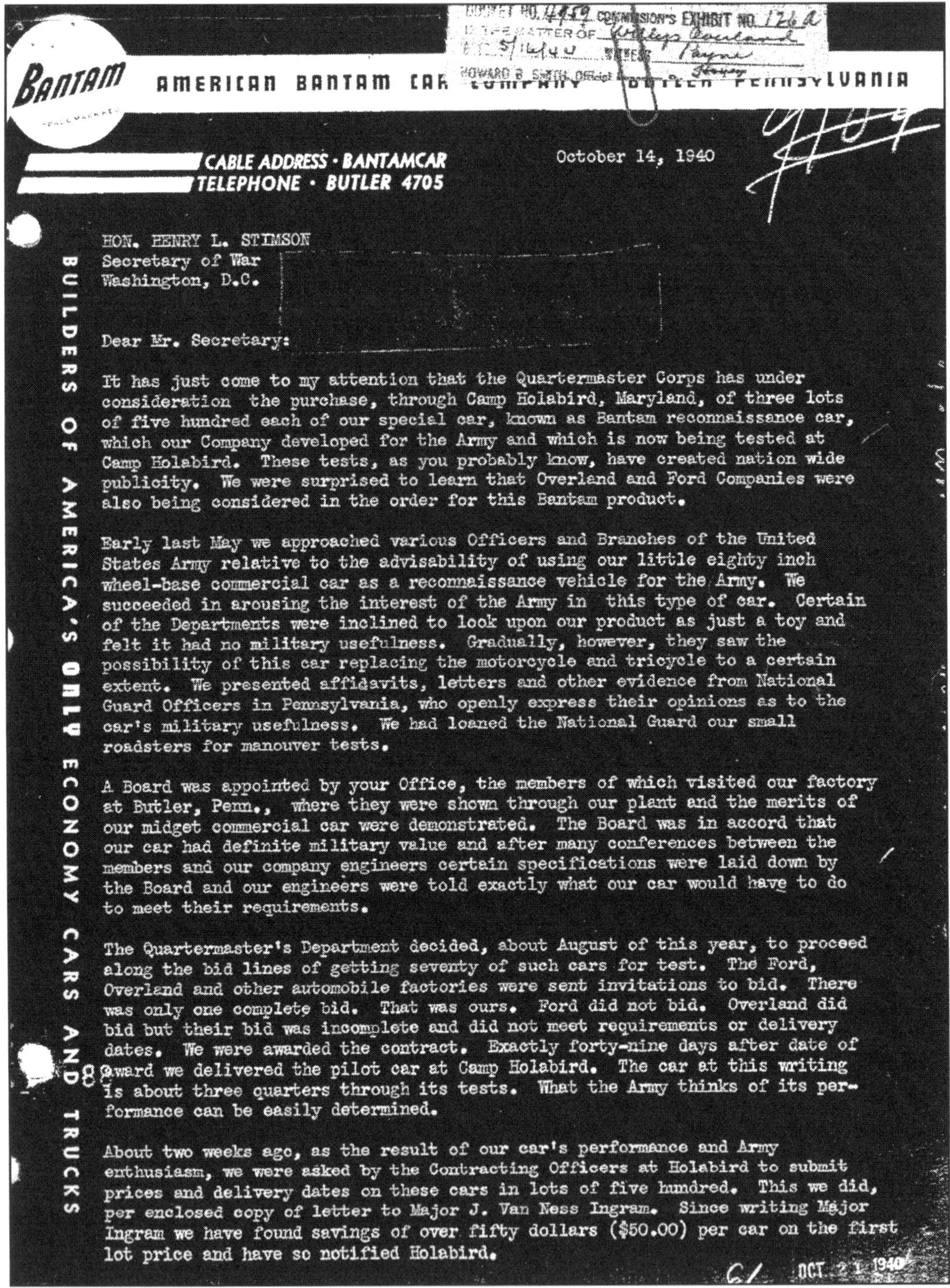

BANTAM

AMERICAN BANTAM CAR COMPANY BUTLER PENNSYLVANIA

CABLE ADDRESS · BANTAMCAR
TELEPHONE · BUTLER 4705

BUILDERS OF AMERICA'S ONLY ECONOMY CARS AND TRUCKS

October 14, 1940

HON. HENRY L. STIMSON
Secretary of War
Washington, D.C.

Dear Mr. Secretary:

It has just come to my attention that the Quartermaster Corps has under consideration the purchase, through Camp Holabird, Maryland, of three lots of five hundred each of our special car, known as Bantam reconnaissance car, which our Company developed for the Army and which is now being tested at Camp Holabird. These tests, as you probably know, have created nation wide publicity. We were surprised to learn that Overland and Ford Companies were also being considered in the order for this Bantam product.

Early last May we approached various Officers and Branches of the United States Army relative to the advisability of using our little eighty inch wheel-base commercial car as a reconnaissance vehicle for the Army. We succeeded in arousing the interest of the Army in this type of car. Certain of the Departments were inclined to look upon our product as just a toy and felt it had no military usefulness. Gradually, however, they saw the possibility of this car replacing the motorcycle and tricycle to a certain extent. We presented affidavits, letters and other evidence from National Guard Officers in Pennsylvania, who openly express their opinions as to the car's military usefulness. We had loaned the National Guard our small roadsters for manouver tests.

A Board was appointed by your Office, the members of which visited our factory at Butler, Penn., where they were shown through our plant and the merits of our midget commercial car were demonstrated. The Board was in accord that our car had definite military value and after many conferences between the members and our company engineers certain specifications were laid down by the Board and our engineers were told exactly what our car would have to do to meet their requirements.

The Quartermaster's Department decided, about August of this year, to proceed along the bid lines of getting seventy of such cars for test. The Ford, Overland and other automobile factories were sent invitations to bid. There was only one complete bid. That was ours. Ford did not bid. Overland did bid but their bid was incomplete and did not meet requirements or delivery dates. We were awarded the contract. Exactly forty-nine days after date of award we delivered the pilot car at Camp Holabird. The car at this writing is about three quarters through its tests. What the Army thinks of its performance can be easily determined.

About two weeks ago, as the result of our car's performance and Army enthusiasm, we were asked by the Contracting Officers at Holabird to submit prices and delivery dates on these cars in lots of five hundred. This we did, per enclosed copy of letter to Major J. Van Ness Ingram. Since writing Major Ingram we have found savings of over fifty dollars ($50.00) per car on the first lot price and have so notified Holabird.

OCT 21 1940

Shocked when Bantam first realized they would have competition to produce the new vehicle, Charles Payne sent a scathing letter to Secretary of War Stimson. By going "all the way to the top" the Butler firm engendered great animosity from the Quartermaster Corps. This would haunt them for the rest of the Jeep procurement. In the end, Bantam did not have the resources to fulfill the Army's production needs.

Source: United States National Archives, College Park, Maryland

Ford's October 16th Quote

Ford Motor Company

FACTORY AND GENERAL OFFICES
DEARBORN, MICH.

ALEXANDRIA, VA.

Lieut Col J Van Ness Ingram
Purchasing & Contracting Officer
Holabird Quartermaster Depot
Baltimore Maryland

October 16, 1940

FEDERAL TRADE COMMISSION
DOCKET NO. 4959 COMMISSION'S EXHIBIT NO. 112 E
IN THE MATTER OF Willys Overland
DATE 5/15/44 WITNESS
HOWARD B. SMITH, Official Reporter; By Hoyez

Sir:

In response to your recent request we submit herewith a quotation of $1180.00 each f.o.b. Dearborn, Mich., for 500 Light Reconnaissance and Command Cars (4-wheel drive 2-wheel steer) Conforming to specifications accompanying Invitation 398-41-9, dated July 11, 1940. It is understood that, along the lines of our discussion with you this morning, this quotation is subject to our reaching a mutual agreement regarding several variations from the above specifications, such as, but not limited to, vehicle weight, body details, etc.

The above price is subject to a cash discount of $50.00 per vehicle for payment within 30 days from date of delivery or date of receipt of our voucher. Vouchers will be submitted for quantities of 50 units, and payment is to be made against these vouchers.

Prices quoted do not include any Federal taxes from which exemption is granted, or as to which a credit or refund is provided for, nor any tax imposed by a state, county or municipality upon the transaction of this procurement of these materials. It is understood that the necessary tax exemption certificates will be supplied us to cover.

This quotation is open for acceptance for 30 days from this date.

We will deliver pilot model within 45 days from date of receipt of official award. Delivery will be made at the rate of 50 vehicles per week starting 16 weeks after receipt of order; provided, however, that due allowance shall be made for time required for test and approval of pilot model.

Respectfully,
FORD MOTOR COMPANY
H C Cunningham
Manager

HMC:S

14.

Ford responded to the request for quotes on October 16, 1940, stating a price of $1,180.00 per vehicle.

Source: United States National Archives, College Park, Maryland

Rice's October 18th Quote

After receiving Willys' October 8th quote, representatives of the Quartermaster Corps. contacted them and told them if they wished to be considered they, "had better sharpen their pencils." Rice responded on October 18th with a new price of $1,195.00 per vehicle for the 500 cars.

Willys Quad - Subject of Rice's Quote. Source: United States National Archives, College Park, Maryland

Army Orders from All 3 Companies

FEDERAL TRADE COMMISSION
DOCKET NO. 4959 COMMISSION'S EXHIBIT NO. 117 E
IN THE MATTER OF Willys Overland
5/15/44 WITNESS
HOWARD B. SMITH, Official Reporter; By Hoyer

In view of the fact that certain minor changes may be required in the development of the vehicle involving increase in prices, it is believed that $1,250.00 is a fair estimate of the maximum cost of each vehicle, if procured in lots of five hundred (500) from each manufacturer. Accordingly, this price restriction should be imposed in negotiations with manufacturers.

Conclusions: It is the conclusion of the Committee that for the proper development of the project of a light (4x4) truck for command and reconnaissance purposes, and to facilitate mass production possibilities fifteen hundred (1,500) additional vehicles should be procured at once on a negotiated basis of five hundred (500) each from the Bantam Car, Willys-Overland and Ford Companies.

Recommendations: It is recommended that:

(1) The project for development and service test of seventy (70) trucks, ¼-ton, (4x4) for command and reconnaissance purposes be extended immediately to include fifteen hundred (1,500) additional vehicles.

(2) The Quartermaster General be authorized to execute negotiated contracts with the Bantam Car Company, the Willys-Overland Company and the Ford Company for five hundred (500) vehicles each, at unit cost not to exceed $1,250.00.

(3) Should a manufacturer fail to meet this price limitation the negotiation be made for fifteen hundred (1,500) vehicles divided equally amongst the manufacturers meeting this limitation.

(4) The Quartermaster General be authorized immediately to notify the Spicer Manufacturing Company of the War Department's intention to contract for fifteen hundred (1,500) vehicles and guarantee them an outlet for fifteen hundred (1,500) sets of axles and transfer cases.

J. H. Johnson
J. H. JOHNSON, Lt. Col., QMC,
Chairman.

Non-concurrence, See Special Com.
W. F. LEE,
Lieut. Colonel, Infantry.

G. X. Cheves
G. X. CHEVES,
Lieut. Colonel, Cavalry.

Non-concurrence See Memo attached
J. W. MacKelvie
J. W. MacKELVIE,
Lieut. Colonel, F. A.

See Special Concurrence attached.
R. L. HOWZE,
Captain, Cavalry.

7 Incls.
Incl. 1 - Ltr. Hol.QMD, 10-17-40.
" 2 - 2 Ltrs. Ford Motor Co. 10-16-40.
" 3 - Ltr.Willys-Overland Motors,Inc.10-8-40.
" 4 - 2 Ltrs.Amer.Bantam Car Co. 10-4-40 & 10-9-40.
" 5 - Non-concurrence,Chief Inf. 10-21-40.
" 6 - Non-Concurrence,Chief F.A. 10-21-40.
Incl.7-Special Concurrence Chief Cav. 10-21-40.

-2-

On October 18, 1940, the QMC Motor Transport Sub-Committee of the Quartermaster Corps. Technical Committee approved Bantam for the 70 units from the first contract as well as authorizing 500 each from Bantam, Willys, and Ford.

Source: United States National Archives, College Park, Maryland

Infantry Objects

FEDERAL TRADE COMMISSION
DOCKET NO. 4959 COMMISSION'S EXHIBIT NO. 117
IN THE MATTER OF Willys Overland
DATE 5/19/41 WITNESS
HOWARD B. SMITH, Official Reporter; By

WAR DEPARTMENT
OFFICE OF THE CHIEF OF INFANTRY
WASHINGTON

October 21, 1940.

SUBJECT: Non-concurrence in Proceedings of Motor Transport Sub-committee of Quartermaster Corps Technical Committee, Dated October 18, 1940.

TO: The Quartermaster General.

(THRU: The Chairman, Quartermaster Technical Committee.)

1. The representative of the Chief of Infantry is unable to concur in the conclusions and recommendations the majority, for the following reasons:

a. The program recommended will not provide the number of these vehicles needed by the Infantry in lieu of the motorcycle with side-car, procurement of which is in suspense, pending the adoption of a substitute.

b. The procedure adopted will inevitably result in delay beyond that justified at this time.

c. Since, at the present time, as stated in the majority report, there is only one source available for the supply of the axles and transfer cases, and since these are the only ones essentially distinguishing this vehicle from vehicles heretofore available in this general class, the proposed apportioning of the procurement among three manufacturers will not, to any considerable extent, extend the field of development. It may, on the contrary, result in restricting the field, since it is understood that failure on the part of the government to support the manufacturer who has developed this vehicle with adequate contracts may result in the elimination of that source entirely.

d. The purchase, from the Overland and Ford, of a total of one thousand vehicles which have never been seen, much less tested, is not justified, in view of the fact that a vehicle has been engineered, thoroughly tested, and found satisfactory. The adequate testing of a tactical vehicle, from the view-point of the using arms, is a lengthy procedure. Perfunctory testing is not satisfactory. The

-1-

Incl # 5.

A number of using Arms, in particular the Infantry, objected to awarding contracts to Willys and Ford who did not have tested and accepted prototypes. Their objections were overruled. Two of the contributing factors to the decision: Bantam's limited manufacturing capacity and the bugaboo letter from Payne.

Source: United States National Archives, College Park, Maryland

General Joseph E. Barzynski

General Joseph E. Barzynski, as Gregory's right-hand man, would provide overall coordination for the Jeep procurement.

General Joseph E. Barzynski. Source: From the collection of the Polish Museum of America

The AG Weighs In

On October 29, 1940, the Adjutant General chimed in with a decision that all 1,500 vehicles should go to Bantam and none to Willys or Ford because they had not delivered, nor had an accepted prototype.

Adjutant General Emory S. Adams in 1940. Source: Public Domain

The Quartermaster Objects

FEDERAL TRADE COMMISSION
DOCKET NO. 4959 COMMISSION'S EXHIBIT NO. 1172
IN THE MATTER OF Willys Overland
DATE 7/15/44 WITNESS
HOWARD B. SMITH, Official Reporter, by Hoyez

QM 451 M-P (Proc. 398-41-9)
(Trucks, ¼-Ton 4 x 4) 2nd Ind.
War Department, OQMG, Washington, November 1, 1940. To: The Adjutant General.

1. Reconsideration of the action directed in paragraph 3, 1st Ind. is requested based upon the following:

a. The fact that information about the action directed was conveyed to Mr. Charles H. Payne, Assistant to the President and Washington Sales Representative of the American Bantam Car Company in time for him to convey this information to the Holabird Quartermaster Depot and to the representatives there of the Ford Motor Company and the Willys-Overland Motors, Incorporated, on Friday, October 25th, although the Quartermaster General's office did not receive official notification until October 30th has adversely affected vendor relations which are important to the proper procurement of motor vehicles.

b. The original proposal to extend the project for development and service test from 70 to 1570 and to divide the order for 1500 additional trucks between two or three companies was a carefully considered plan initiated by the office of the Quartermaster General, so as to insure the proper engineering development, and, in addition, the development of adequate productive facilities to produce this type of car in the quantities that may be needed, and such a carefully considered program should not be upset unless there are other extremely serious considerations involved.

c. The representatives of the Willys-Overland Company and the Ford Motor Company were called in and encouraged to make major expenditures for engineering development work, after telephonic consultation and verbal approval of Colonel Aurand to the Commanding Officer of the Holabird Quartermaster Depot.

d. The probable requirements of this vehicle are not less than 11,800 for procurement before June 30, 1941, in the event that the service test proves these vehicles satisfactory. It is extremely desirable that adequate and competitive sources of production be developed for this vehicle. It is the considered opinion of the Quartermaster General's office that the American Bantam Car Company cannot furnish these requirements and insure a continuing service organization. Note that the American Bantam Car Company wanted an advance payment of approximately thirty per cent or $52,000 on the original contract for seventy-two cars. Note also the following extract from paragraph 1.c of the communication of the Infantry representative of October 21, 1940: " . . it is understood that failure on the part of the government to support the manufacturer who has developed this vehicle with adequate contracts may result in the elimination of that source entirely."

-5-

The Quartermaster Corp. would vigorously object to the AG's decision. Gregory penned a long missive, dated November 1, 1940, that argued for the three-vendor approach and severely criticized Bantam, most likely a repercussion from Payne's October 14th letter to Stimson.

Source: United States National Archives, College Park, Maryland

AG Responds To Gregory

The Adjutant General responded on November 5, 1940, dismissing the Quartermaster's arguments and reaffirming the award of 1,500 to Bantam. However, he did leave the door open for Willys and Ford.

A BRC 40 Built Under the Contract for 1,500. Source: Public Domain

Bantam Awarded 1,500

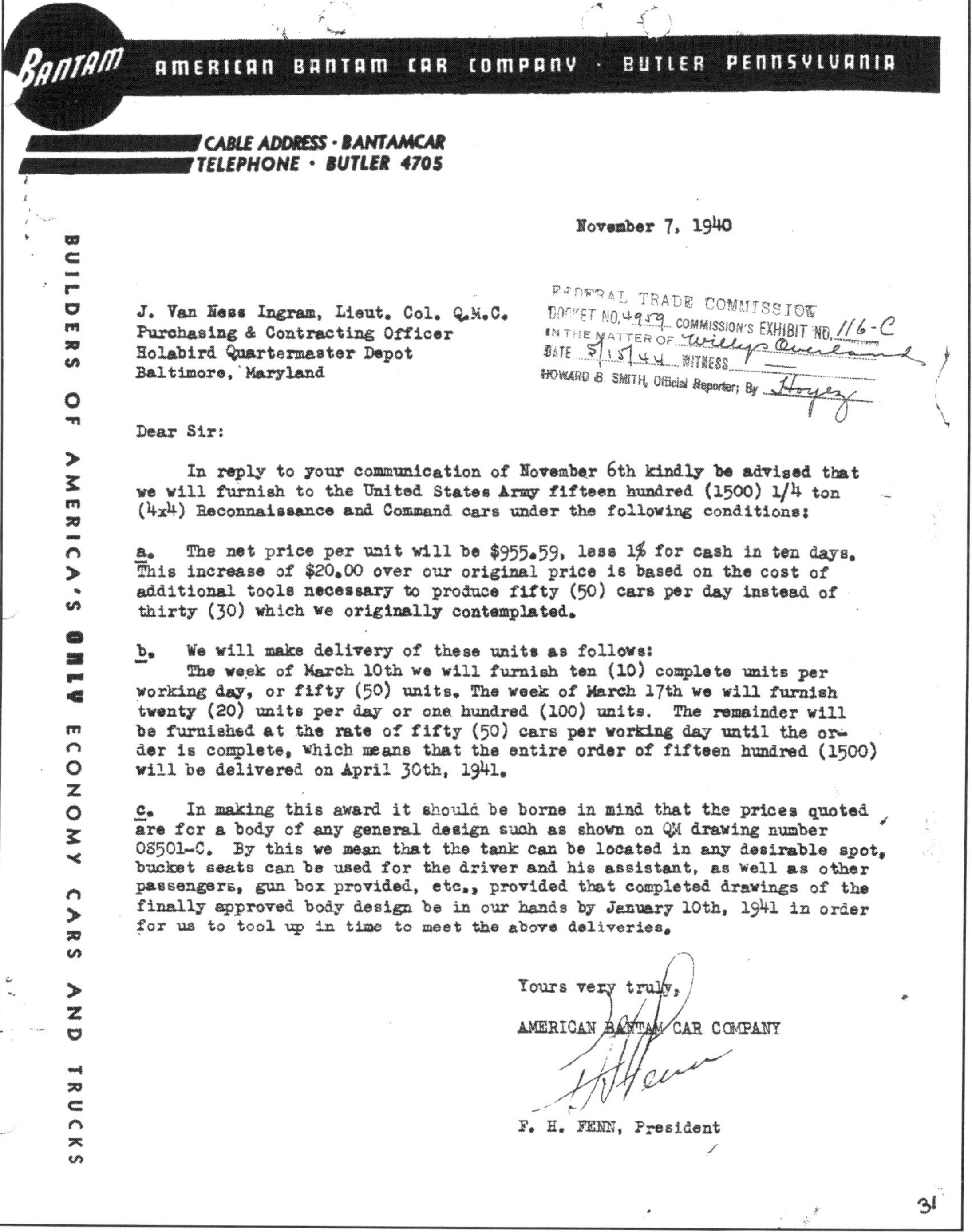

BANTAM AMERICAN BANTAM CAR COMPANY · BUTLER PENNSYLVANIA

CABLE ADDRESS · BANTAMCAR
TELEPHONE · BUTLER 4705

BUILDERS OF AMERICA'S ONLY ECONOMY CARS AND TRUCKS

November 7, 1940

J. Van Ness Ingram, Lieut. Col. Q.M.C.
Purchasing & Contracting Officer
Holabird Quartermaster Depot
Baltimore, Maryland

FEDERAL TRADE COMMISSION
DOCKET NO. 4959 COMMISSION'S EXHIBIT NO. 116-C
IN THE MATTER OF Willys Overland
DATE 5/15/44 WITNESS
HOWARD B. SMITH, Official Reporter; By Hoyez

Dear Sir:

In reply to your communication of November 6th kindly be advised that we will furnish to the United States Army fifteen hundred (1500) 1/4 ton (4x4) Reconnaissance and Command cars under the following conditions:

a. The net price per unit will be $955.59, less 1% for cash in ten days. This increase of $20.00 over our original price is based on the cost of additional tools necessary to produce fifty (50) cars per day instead of thirty (30) which we originally contemplated.

b. We will make delivery of these units as follows:
The week of March 10th we will furnish ten (10) complete units per working day, or fifty (50) units. The week of March 17th we will furnish twenty (20) units per day or one hundred (100) units. The remainder will be furnished at the rate of fifty (50) cars per working day until the order is complete, which means that the entire order of fifteen hundred (1500) will be delivered on April 30th, 1941.

c. In making this award it should be borne in mind that the prices quoted are for a body of any general design such as shown on QM drawing number 08501-C. By this we mean that the tank can be located in any desirable spot, bucket seats can be used for the driver and his assistant, as well as other passengers, gun box provided, etc., provided that completed drawings of the finally approved body design be in our hands by January 10th, 1941 in order for us to tool up in time to meet the above deliveries.

Yours very truly,
AMERICAN BANTAM CAR COMPANY

F. H. FENN, President

31

On November 6, 1940, the Quartermaster notified Bantam of their award for 1,500 vehicles, marking the high water mark for the Butler firm in the procurement. Fenn responded the next day accepting the award.

Source: United States National Archives, College Park, Maryland

Ford's November 9th Quote

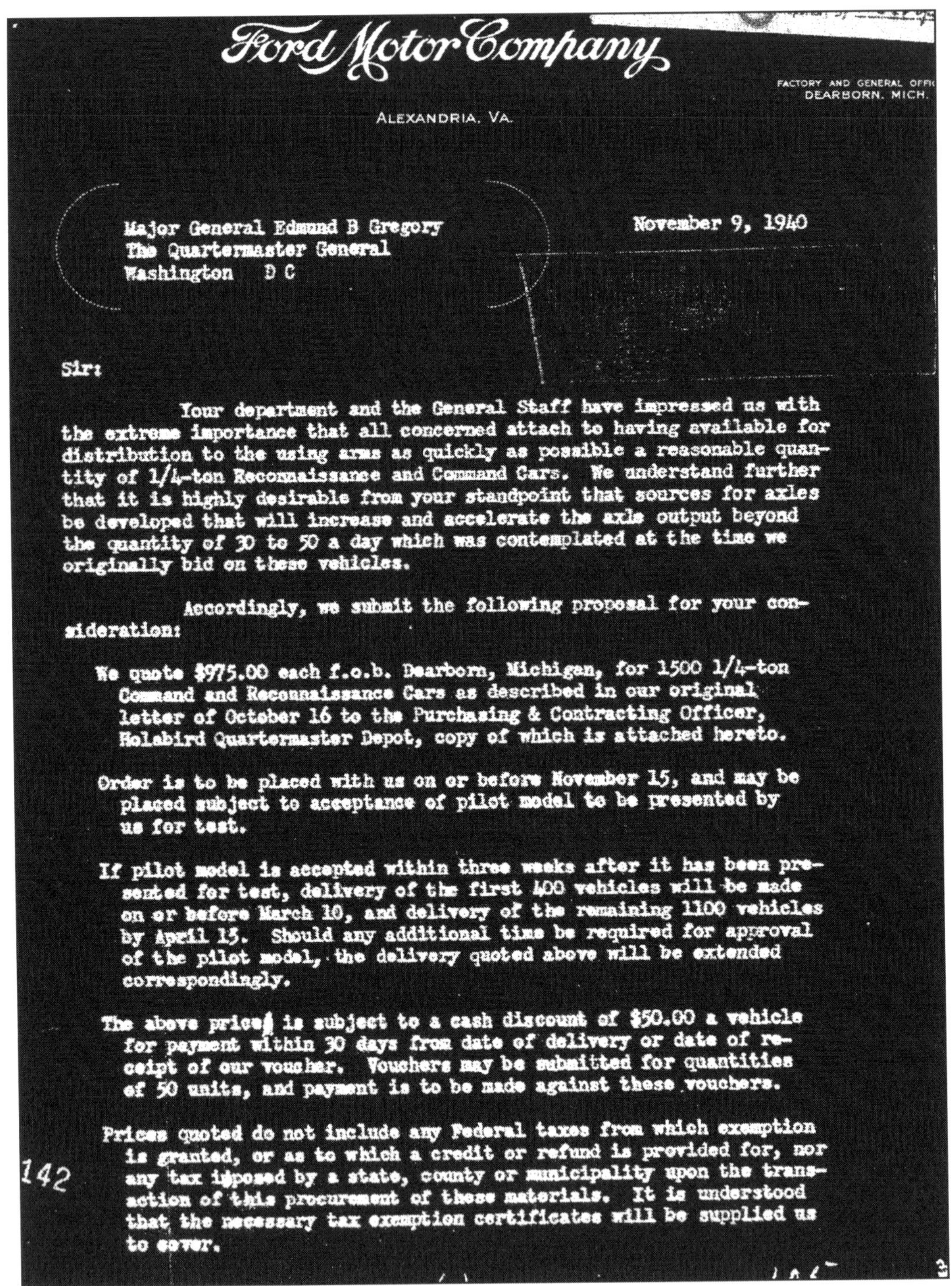

Ford Motor Company

FACTORY AND GENERAL OFFI
DEARBORN, MICH.

ALEXANDRIA, VA.

Major General Edmund B Gregory
The Quartermaster General
Washington D C

November 9, 1940

Sir:

Your department and the General Staff have impressed us with the extreme importance that all concerned attach to having available for distribution to the using arms as quickly as possible a reasonable quantity of 1/4-ton Reconnaissance and Command Cars. We understand further that it is highly desirable from your standpoint that sources for axles be developed that will increase and accelerate the axle output beyond the quantity of 30 to 50 a day which was contemplated at the time we originally bid on these vehicles.

Accordingly, we submit the following proposal for your consideration:

We quote $975.00 each f.o.b. Dearborn, Michigan, for 1500 1/4-ton Command and Reconnaissance Cars as described in our original letter of October 16 to the Purchasing & Contracting Officer, Holabird Quartermaster Depot, copy of which is attached hereto.

Order is to be placed with us on or before November 15, and may be placed subject to acceptance of pilot model to be presented by us for test.

If pilot model is accepted within three weeks after it has been presented for test, delivery of the first 400 vehicles will be made on or before March 10, and delivery of the remaining 1100 vehicles by April 15. Should any additional time be required for approval of the pilot model, the delivery quoted above will be extended correspondingly.

The above price is subject to a cash discount of $50.00 a vehicle for payment within 30 days from date of delivery or date of receipt of our voucher. Vouchers may be submitted for quantities of 50 units, and payment is to be made against these vouchers.

Prices quoted do not include any Federal taxes from which exemption is granted, or as to which a credit or refund is provided for, nor
142 any tax imposed by a state, county or municipality upon the transaction of this procurement of these materials. It is understood that the necessary tax exemption certificates will be supplied us to cover.

Despite the decision to only award Bantam, Ford sent in another quote on November 9, to build 1,500 vehicles. Subsequent events would prove the wisdom of sending the letter.

Source: United States National Archives, College Park, Maryland

National Defense Advisory Commission

At this time while the United States prepared for war, an agency known as the National Defense Advisory Commission had the final say in every defense-related procurement. On November 14, 1940, John Biggers of that organization approved Bantam's award, but also reinstated the three-vendor approach. He awarded orders of 1,500 each to both Willys and Ford!

John D. Biggers. Source: Public Domain

Willys Submits Another Quote

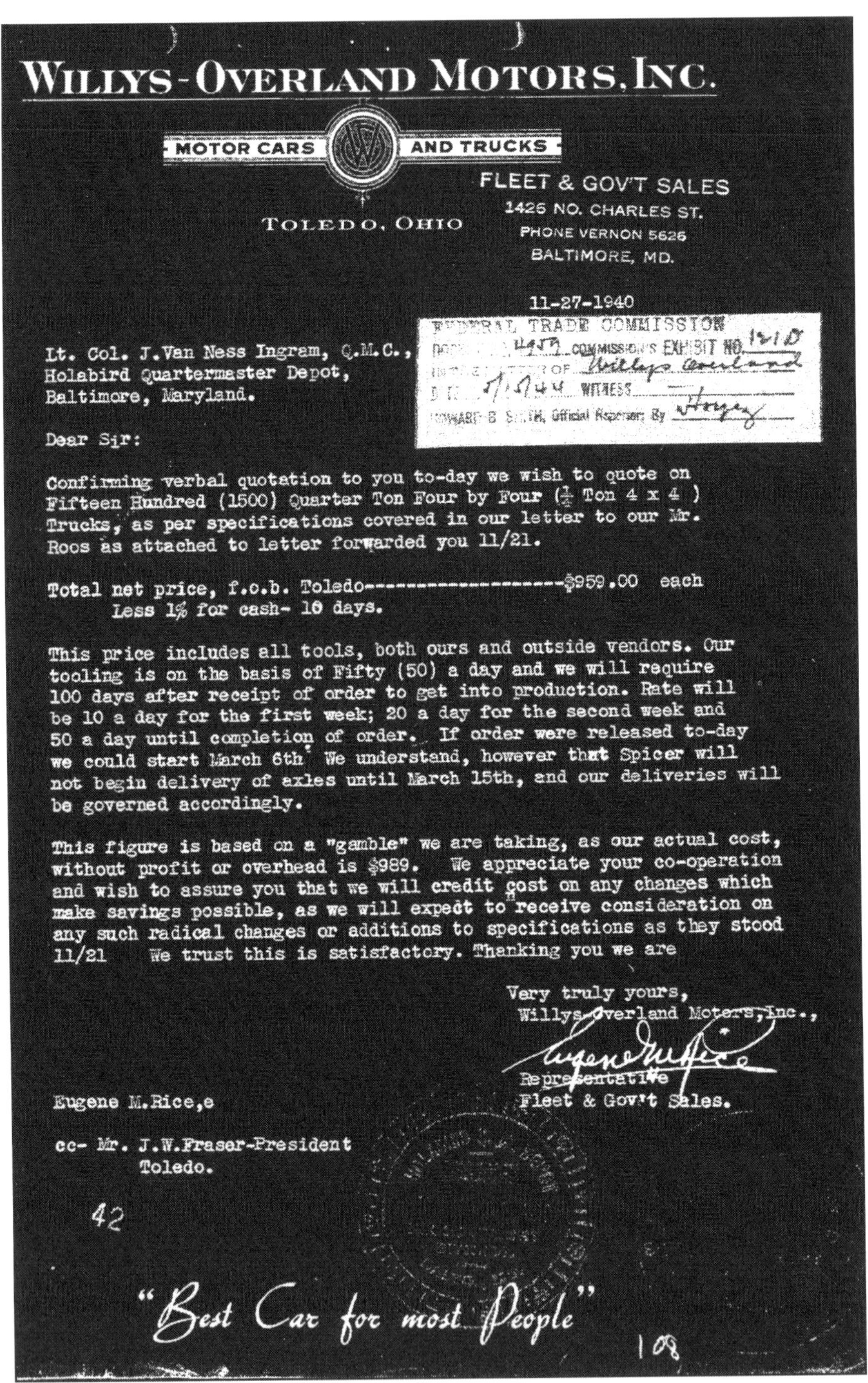

WILLYS-OVERLAND MOTORS, INC.

MOTOR CARS AND TRUCKS

TOLEDO, OHIO

FLEET & GOV'T SALES
1426 NO. CHARLES ST.
PHONE VERNON 5626
BALTIMORE, MD.

11-27-1940

FEDERAL TRADE COMMISSION
COMMISSION'S EXHIBIT NO. 1210
OF Willys Overland
5/5/44 WITNESS
Official Reporter; By

Lt. Col. J. Van Ness Ingram, Q.M.C.,
Holabird Quartermaster Depot,
Baltimore, Maryland.

Dear Sir:

Confirming verbal quotation to you to-day we wish to quote on Fifteen Hundred (1500) Quarter Ton Four by Four (¼ Ton 4 x 4) Trucks, as per specifications covered in our letter to our Mr. Roos as attached to letter forwarded you 11/21.

Total net price, f.o.b. Toledo--------------------$959.00 each
Less 1% for cash- 10 days.

This price includes all tools, both ours and outside vendors. Our tooling is on the basis of Fifty (50) a day and we will require 100 days after receipt of order to get into production. Rate will be 10 a day for the first week; 20 a day for the second week and 50 a day until completion of order. If order were released to-day we could start March 6th. We understand, however that Spicer will not begin delivery of axles until March 15th, and our deliveries will be governed accordingly.

This figure is based on a "gamble" we are taking, as our actual cost, without profit or overhead is $989. We appreciate your co-operation and wish to assure you that we will credit cost on any changes which make savings possible, as we will expect to receive consideration on any such radical changes or additions to specifications as they stood 11/21 We trust this is satisfactory. Thanking you we are

Very truly yours,
Willys-Overland Motors, Inc.,
Eugene M. Rice
Representative
Fleet & Gov't Sales.

Eugene M.Rice,e

cc- Mr. J.W.Fraser-President
Toledo.

42

"Best Car for most People"

108

Following Biggers' decision, by the end of November, Ford's contract for 1,500 went through smoothly. Willys took slightly longer. The Toledo firm submitted one final quote on November 27, 1940. Willys' contract for 1,500 became official in early December.

Source: United States National Archives, College Park, Maryland

CHAPTER 12

Willys and Ford Prototypes are Tested and Accepted

The Willys Quad Undergoing Testing. Source: Public Domain

Testing the Ford Pygmy

Between November 1940 and January 1941, the Pygmy would undergo the same grueling tests as the BRC.

Source: Public Domain

The Pygmy is Accepted

January 6,
1 9 4 1

SUBJECT: Preliminary Report of Pilot Model 1/4 ton, 4 x 4, Ford Truck, Contract Number W-398-qm-8887

TO: Purchasing and Contracting Officer, Holabird Quartermaster Depot, Baltimore, Maryland.

1. The following comments on the inspection of the subject trucks are submitted:

a. Vehicles arrived at this depot November 23, 1940.

PAR. C-4. Tire chains were not submitted with the Pilot Model Vehicle, therefore not possible to check them. It is recommended that a set of chains be forwarded to this depot at the earliest opportunity for proper inspection and for installation on the Pilot Model vehicle.

D-1. Weights:

Front	-	1185
Rear	-	1215
TOTAL	-	2400

Gross Weight:

Front	-	1210
Rear	-	1790
TOTAL	-	3000

Gross weight was taken with a payload of 600 pounds.

D-1b. Ground clearance of rear axle was 7-1/2 inches. Specification requirement is 8-1/2 inches. It is believed that this requirement chan be waived in as much as no difficulties were experienced in all types of operations.

The top portion of the windshield frame was not sufficiently high to permit clear vision to the front. It is understood that this will be raised in accordance with results of test conducted with Mr. Cook of the Ford Company.

- No difficulty was experienced with the frame. The frame was reinforced after 4,395 miles of operation and it is understood that in production, frames

-1-

The Quartermaster completed their tests on the Ford Pygmy and issued their report on January 6, 1941. While issues surfaced, they did not constitute anything that deterred the vehicle's acceptance. Shortly after the car's acceptance, Ford received their approved contract for 1,500 units. Ford would call this allotment of units the "GP"—G for Government and P signifying a wheelbase of eighty inches.

Source: United States Natonal Archives, College Park, Maryland

Testing the Willys Quad

Between November 1940 and January 1941 the Quad would undergo the same grueling tests as the BRC and the Pygmy.

Source: Courtesy of the Patrick Foster Historical Collection

Willys Fails!

Report of Sub-Committee on
Pilot Model Test of Willys
Overland 1/4 Ton, 4x4, Truck,
January 14, 1941.

(4) Windshield: Windshield failure in this case has been due to the use of bronze castings for the windshield hinge support brackets. Bronze castings are used on the pilot model in order to save time. This failure can be eliminated by the use of malleable steel castings on the production vehicles.

(5) Starting Pin: Starting pin failure in this vehicle is due to the starting pin becoming loose. This difficulty has not yet been fully corrected.

c. Weight: The major objection in deviation from specification requirements in the case of the Willys Overland 1/4 Ton, 4x4, Truck is the excessive weight. In this connection, it was pointed out that the Bantam Company originally offered a vehicle of 2,030 pounds, but now has added 130 pounds to make the required 2,160 pounds. Ford has guaranteed to meet the weight limitation of 2,175 pounds. Willys Overland have stated in writing that they will guarantee a weight of 2,300 pounds, and will build down as near to 2,200 pounds as possible. It is believed that in order for Willys Overland to meet the weight limitation of 2,175 lbs., it will be necessary to use a smaller size engine. It was the consensus of opinion of the members of the Sub-Committee present that the maximum weight should not exceed 2,160 pounds without the machine gun base, and with 5.50-16 inch tires, or 2,175 pounds with the machine gun base, and 5.50-16 inch tires.

d. Tires: Opinion was expressed as to the relative merits of tires 6.00-16 inch and tires 5.50-16 inch in size. It was stated that more life but not more performance was secured with the larger tire. It was suggested that all vehicles be ordered with 4-inch rims, 1/2 of the vehicles to be equipped with 5.50-16 inch size tires, and the remainder to be equipped with 6.00-16 inch size tires.

e. Procurement: The Chairman reviewed the correspondence and the directives authorizing the procurement by The Quartermaster General from the Willys Overland Company, the Ford Motor Company, and the American Bantam Company of 1/4 Ton, 4x4, Trucks, including the directive to procure 1,500 vehicles of this type from the Willys Overland Company, after accepted service test. Further discussion was to the effect that, following the usual procedure, when we complete a pilot model test we indicate to the manufacturer the changes necessary to meet specification requirements for a satisfactory vehicle. Generally speaking, the Willys Overland 1/4 Ton, 4x4, Truck is considered as possible of correction to a satisfactory vehicle, provided the weight can be reduced to not to exceed 2,160 pounds without machine gun base plate and with 5.50-16 inch tires. The smaller engine offers the only method of reducing the weight. The Ford Motor Company and the American Bantam Company have produced vehicles according to the standards laid down, including changes indicated by the pilot model test to be necessary. However, the

-2-

In a stunning reversal of fortune at a meeting held on January 14, 1941, the Motor Transport Sub-Committee of the Quartermaster Corps. Technical Committee rejected the Quad. The test reports cited significant problems with the vehicle's weight the most egregious.

Source: United States National Archives, College Park, Maryland

Willys Responds

The committee's decision set off a firestorm. Eugene Rice, on Willys' behalf, similar to Charles Payne in October 1940, went right to the top. He wired Chief of Staff Marshall on January 21, 1941 to plead his case. His wire was received at the Signal Corps. station in room 3411, Munitions Building, Washington, DC.

Source: Public Domain

Marshall Responds

Chief of Staff Marshall referred the Willys matter to the Adjutant General. The AG ruled the committee's actions as justified and notified the Toledo firm of this decision on January 28, 1941. At the moment, Willys remained out of the Jeep procurement with apparently no cards left to play.

Source: United States National Archives, College Park, Maryland

Barzynski Pleads Willys' Case

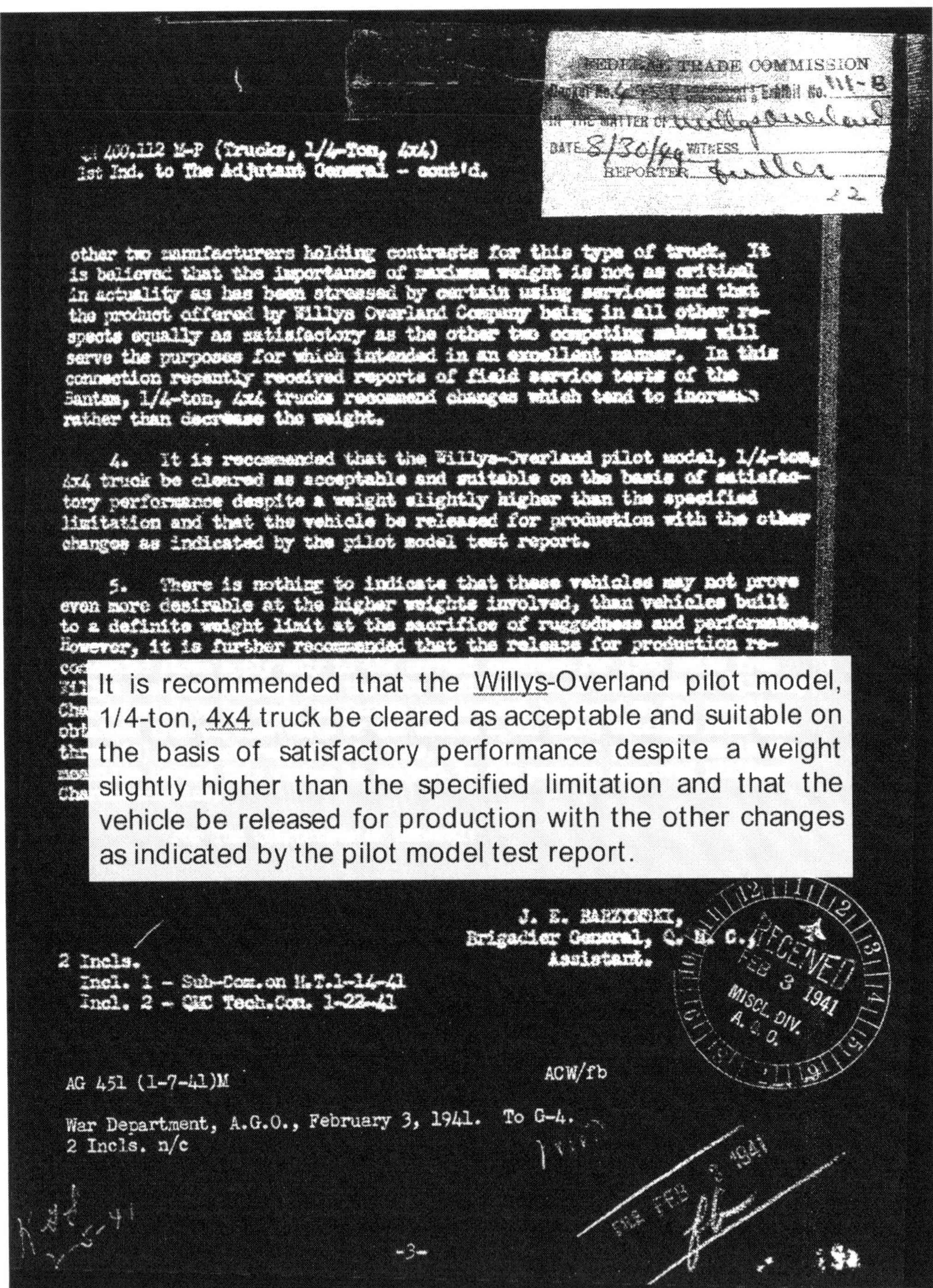

FEDERAL TRADE COMMISSION
IN THE MATTER OF
DATE 8/30/44 WITNESS
REPORTER

QM 400.112 M-P (Trucks, 1/4-Ton, 4x4)
1st Ind. to The Adjutant General - cont'd.

other two manufacturers holding contracts for this type of truck. It is believed that the importance of maximum weight is not as critical in actuality as has been stressed by certain using services and that the product offered by Willys Overland Company being in all other respects equally as satisfactory as the other two competing makes will serve the purposes for which intended in an excellent manner. In this connection recently received reports of field service tests of the Bantam, 1/4-ton, 4x4 trucks recommend changes which tend to increase rather than decrease the weight.

4. It is recommended that the Willys-Overland pilot model, 1/4-ton, 4x4 truck be cleared as acceptable and suitable on the basis of satisfactory performance despite a weight slightly higher than the specified limitation and that the vehicle be released for production with the other changes as indicated by the pilot model test report.

5. There is nothing to indicate that these vehicles may not prove even more desirable at the higher weights involved, than vehicles built to a definite weight limit at the sacrifice of ruggedness and performance. However, it is further recommended that the release for production re-

It is recommended that the Willys-Overland pilot model, 1/4-ton, 4x4 truck be cleared as acceptable and suitable on the basis of satisfactory performance despite a weight slightly higher than the specified limitation and that the vehicle be released for production with the other changes as indicated by the pilot model test report.

J. E. BARZYNSKI,
Brigadier General, Q. M. C.,
Assistant.

2 Incls.
Incl. 1 - Sub-Com.on M.T.1-14-41
Incl. 2 - QMC Tech.Com. 1-22-41

RECEIVED FEB 3 1941 MISCL. DIV. A. G. O.

AG 451 (1-7-41)M

ACW/fb

War Department, A.G.O., February 3, 1941. To G-4.
2 Incls. n/c

FEB 3 1941

-3-

In a remarkable action, General Barzynski wrote a memo to both the Adjutant General and the Chief of Staff's office pleading Willys' case.

Source: United States National Archives, College Park, Maryland

Willys Approved After All!

Completing the stunning turn of events...
After receiving Barzynski's memo, both the Chief of Staff's Office and the Adjutant General reversed course. Willys had both of their offices' approvals by February 8, 1941.

Source: United States National Archives, College Park, Maryland

Willys Accepted

HEADQUARTERS
HOLABIRD QUARTERMASTER DEPOT
BALTIMORE, MARYLAND

In reply refer to:
P-Adm

February 11, 1941.

SUBJECT: Contract No. W-398-qm-8888

FEDERAL TRADE COMMISSION
DOCKET NO. 4959 RESPONDENT'S EXHIBIT NO. 3
IN THE MATTER OF Willys Overland
DATE 5/11/44 WITNESS Ingram
HOWARD B. SMITH, Official Reporter; By Hoyes

Willys-Overland Motors, Inc.,
Toledo, Ohio.

Gentlemen:

With further reference to our letter of February 8, 1941, you are informed that, inasmuch as the pilot model vehicle submitted in connection with the subject contract has satisfactorily completed tests with exception of the failure to meet the weight limitation of 2160 pounds, and that the performance of the vehiclein spite of the added weight has been in all respects, equal to that required by the specifications, that your pilot model is accepted as suitable for military usage. It is, therefore released for production with the other changes as indicated by the pilot model inspection report dated January 8, 1941.

Any modification or revision in the specifications covering future procurements will be based on the results obtained in the service tests of the three makes of vehicles now under procurement.

Very truly yours,

J. VAN NESS INGRAM
Lieut. Colonel, Q.M. Corps.,
Purchasing & Contracting Officer.

JVNI:amc

cc to: Mr. Eugene M. Rice,
Baltimore, Md.

Willys received final approval of the Quartermaster's acceptance on February 11, 1941. Once again the Toledo manufacturer had survived a near-death experience in the Jeep procurement.

Source: United States National Archives, College Park, Maryland

The Willys MA is Born

Willys now had to retool its pilot based upon the tests reports and Army feedback from the technical committee. While it would take painstaking effort, the Toledo firm corrected all the issues, including the weight, by May 1941. They renamed the vehicle the "MA", M for military version, and A for the first model.

Source: Public Domain

CHAPTER 13

1941—The Year of Testing

Balanced on 2 wheels.
Vehicle pulled out easily.

Willys Jeep in Testing–1941. Source: United States National Archives, College Park, Maryland

Infantry Tests the BRC

Early in 1941 the Infantry conducted field tests on the first Bantam models. The "real world" examination of the Bantam, Ford and Willys models would show the versatility, ruggedness, and overall ability of this amazing new vehicle.

Source: United States National Archives, College Park, Maryland

Infantry Tests the BRC (2)

The BRC demonstrating its cross-country ability.

Source: United States National Archives, College Park, Maryland

Infantry Tests the BRC (3)

A steep hill. No problem!

Source: United States National Archives, College Park, Maryland

War in North Africa

The war expanded to North Africa during 1940. Fighting continued in that theater throughout 1941. The final defeat of the Germans on that continent would not come until May 1943. In the photo above, British troops on a Matilda tank fly the Italian flag as they enter Tobruk in January 1941.

Source: Public Domain

Infantry Tests the BRC (4)

The infantry had searched in vain since World War I for a light mobile vehicle that could act as a weapons carrier. The Jeep met that requirement and more!

Source: United States National Archives, College Park, Maryland

Later Testing (1)

The Jeep testing would continue throughout 1941. Pictured above some later models form a convoy.

Source: United States National Archives, College Park, Maryland

Later Testing (2)

Later models preparing to move out.

Source: United States National Archives, College Park, Maryland

Invasion of the Balkans

Germany would invade the Balkans in support of Italy in April 1941. The entire region would succumb to the Axis by June 1, 1941. Pictured above: Australian gunners fighting in Greece.

Source: Public Domain

Summary of Testing (1)

A side-by-side comparison of all three models.

Source: United States National Archives, College Park, Maryland

Summary of Testing (2)

THE FIELD ARTILLERY BOARD
FORT BRAGG, N. C.
Neg. No. 93d-1941 Date 8-23-1941
EXHIBIT D FILE NO. 451.2/K
TEST NO. Q-41-I
1/4-Ton. 4x4. 2-Wheel-Steer. Trucks

All models with the top up!

Source: United States National Archives, College Park, Maryland

Summary of Testing (3)

By the early fall 1941, the Army knew it had a winner on its hands. All three vendors' vehicles proved to be excellent models of the Jeep.

Source: United States National Archives, College Park, Maryland

CHAPTER 14

An RFP for 16,000 Jeeps, Willys' MB, Ford Reemerges

Cartoon by Bill Mauldin. Source: Public Domain

Operation Barbarossa

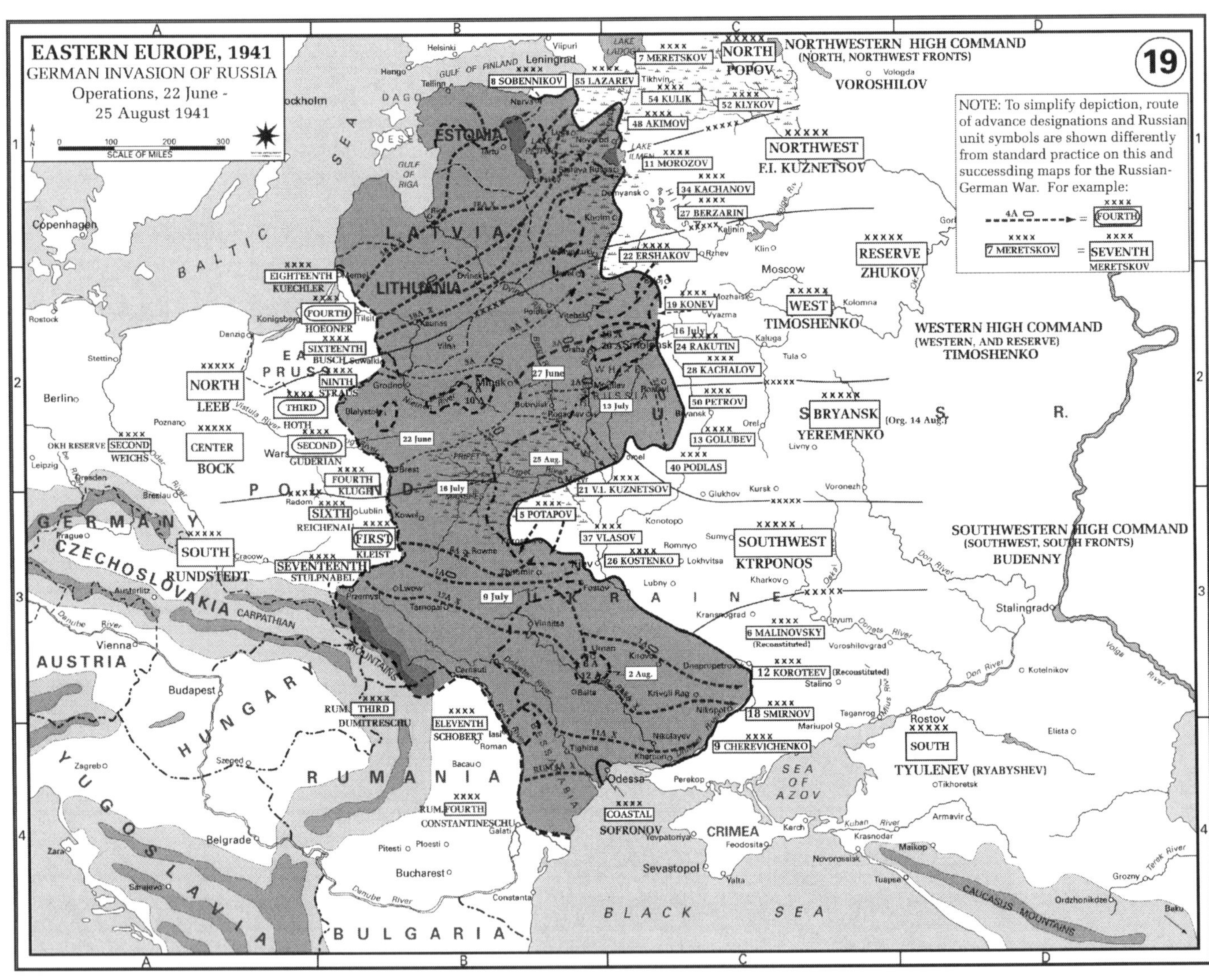

On June 22, 1941, Germany invaded the Soviet Union dramatically expanding the war. Hitler's action added even more urgency to procuring vast quantities of Jeeps.

Source: Public Domain

Meetings to Finalize Jeep Specs

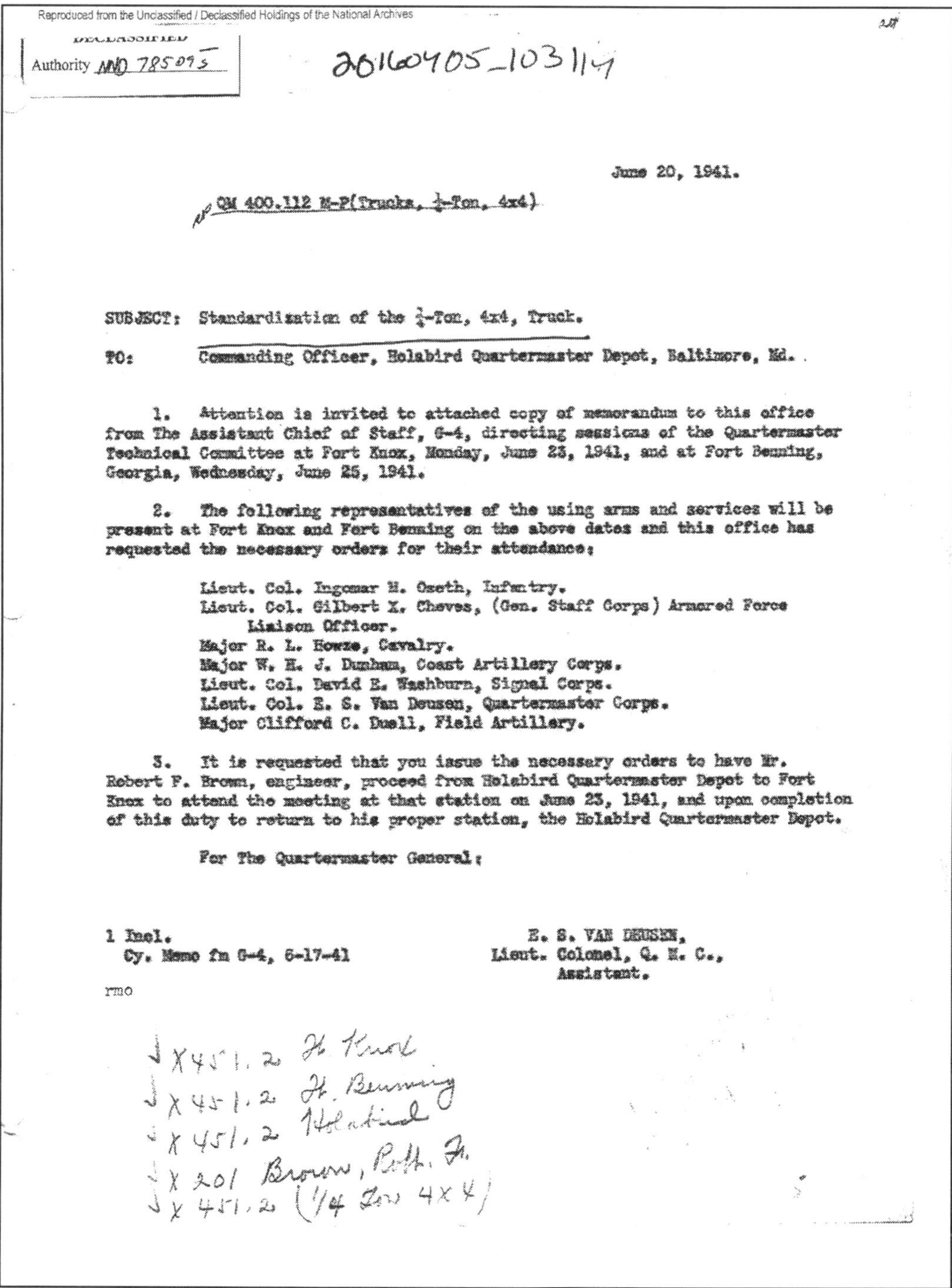

20160405_103114

June 20, 1941.

QM 400.112 M-P(Trucks, ¼-Ton, 4x4)

SUBJECT: Standardization of the ¼-Ton, 4x4, Truck.

TO: Commanding Officer, Holabird Quartermaster Depot, Baltimore, Md.

1. Attention is invited to attached copy of memorandum to this office from The Assistant Chief of Staff, G-4, directing sessions of the Quartermaster Technical Committee at Fort Knox, Monday, June 23, 1941, and at Fort Benning, Georgia, Wednesday, June 25, 1941.

2. The following representatives of the using arms and services will be present at Fort Knox and Fort Benning on the above dates and this office has requested the necessary orders for their attendance:

Lieut. Col. Ingomar M. Oseth, Infantry.
Lieut. Col. Gilbert X. Cheves, (Gen. Staff Corps) Armored Force Liaison Officer.
Major R. L. Howze, Cavalry.
Major W. H. J. Dunham, Coast Artillery Corps.
Lieut. Col. David E. Washburn, Signal Corps.
Lieut. Col. E. S. Van Deusen, Quartermaster Corps.
Major Clifford C. Duell, Field Artillery.

3. It is requested that you issue the necessary orders to have Mr. Robert F. Brown, engineer, proceed from Holabird Quartermaster Depot to Fort Knox to attend the meeting at that station on June 23, 1941, and upon completion of this duty to return to his proper station, the Holabird Quartermaster Depot.

For The Quartermaster General:

1 Incl.
Cy. Memo fm G-4, 6-17-41

E. S. VAN DEUSEN,
Lieut. Colonel, Q. M. C.,
Assistant.

rmo

X 451.2 F. Knox
X 451.2 F. Benning
X 451.2 Holabird
X 201 Brown, Robt. F.
X 451.2 (1/4 Ton 4X4)

In late June 1941, the Quartermaster scheduled two meetings to finalize the specifications for the Jeep. Note that the memo came from Colonel Van Deusen, who ordered Colonel Oseth to attend. He also required the participation of Robert Brown, who on June 19, 1940, drew the first sketch that became the Jeep.

Source: United States National Archives, College Park, Maryland

Final Jeep Specifications

U. S. ARMY
TENTATIVE SPECIFICATION

USA-LP-91-997A.
July 7, 1941.
Superseding:
USA-LP-91-997
June 19, 1941.

TRUCK, 1/4-TON
MOTOR, GASOLINE
(FOUR WHEELS---FOUR WHEEL DRIVE)

A. APPLICABLE SPECIFICATIONS.

A-1. The following current specifications and drawings in effect on date of Invitation for Bids, shall form a part of this specification:

Federal Specification KKK-T-706, Trucks, Motor; Gasoline (Four Wheels-Four Wheel Drive).
Federal Specification ZZ-T-381, Tires; Automobile and Motorcycle, Pneumatic.
Federal Specification ZZ-T-721, Tubes; Automobile and Motorcycle, Inner.
Federal Specification CCC-D-746, Cotton Duck; Fire Resistant.
Q.M. Specification ES-No. 422, Tool Sets - Motor Vehicles.
Q.M. Specification ES-No. 459, General Requirements for Truck, Motor, Gasoline.
Q.M. Specification ES-No. 474, Enamel, Synthetic, Olive Drab, Lusterless.
Q.M. Specification ES-No. 495, Oil and Fuel Tubing, Metallic and Non-Metallic Type.
Q.M. Specification ES-No. 565, Oil Filter.
Q.M. Specification ES-No. 510, Enamel, Synthetic, Stenciling, Lusterless, Various Colors.
Q.M. Specification ES-No. 512, Storage Battery.
Q.M. Specification ES-No. 603, Ignition Suppression.
Rock Island Arsenal Specification RIXS-114, Tubes, Inner, Bullet Seal.
Q.M. Drawing 08366-W, Auxiliary Fuel Filter.
Q.M. Drawing 08480-W, Strap Safety Belt.
Q.M. Drawing 08592-V, Fuel Tank Filler and Cap.
Q.M. Drawing 08593-W, Radiator Filler, Neck, and Cap.
Q.M. Drawing 08634-X, Rear View Mirrors.
Q.M. Drawing 08636-V, Oil Pan Drain Plug and Gasket.
Q.M. Drawing 08641-W, Standard 6-Volt Horn.
Q.M. Drawing 08642-W, Reflex Reflector.
Q.M. Drawing 08660-X, Instrument Board Controls.
Q.M. Drawing 08674-W, Ignition Switch.
Q.M. Drawing 08675-X, Wiring and Lighting System Diagram.
Q.M. Drawing 08677-Y, Panel Instruments.
Q.M. Drawing 08773-V, Stop Light Switch.
Q.M. Drawing 08783-X, Pintle.
Q.M. Drawing 08795-Y, Wheel Assembly, Mounting Studs and Cap Nuts.
Q.M. Drawing 08825-Z, Chassis Outline Assembly and Body.

A-2. Responsibility for obtaining copies of the latest revisions of specifications and drawings listed under A-1. rests with prospective bidders.

B. GENERAL.

B-1. Q.M. Specification ES-No. 459 applies.

C. SERVICE REQUIREMENTS.

C-1. General. The trucks described

The committee met and worked to complete the document which became official on July 7, 1941.

Source: United States National Archives, College Park, Maryland

RFP for 16,000 Jeeps

In a bold decision, the Army decided to issue an RFP for 16,000 Jeeps —a winner takes all contract, even before they completed the testing on the three vendors' vehicles. Note that this RFP went out almost one year to the day of the original RFP, the one they awarded to Bantam. The dedicated Butler crew then built the world-history-changing prototype BRC in 49 days.

Source: Public Domain

Vendor Bid Response

No. 398-42-NEG-1

QMC FORM OF INFORMAL BID (NEGOTIATED CONTRACT) Sheet No. 1a.

ORIGINAL) DUPLICATE) TRIPLICATE) Indicate which by erasure.

DATE OF RECEIPT OF THIS BID

10:00 A. M., July 21 (Eastern Standard Time)

FEDERAL TRADE COMMISSION
DOCKET NO. 4959 EXHIBIT NO. 79-B
IN THE MATTER OF Willys-Overland
DATE 8/7/44 WITNESS —
ELECTREPORTER, INC., Official Reporter
W.M.

To Purchasing & Contracting Officer,
Holabird Quartermaster Depot,
Baltimore, Maryland.

In compliance with your request for informal bids to furnish materials and supplies listed on the reverse hereof or on the accompanying schedules, numbered: Sheets No. 1b. and U.S. Army Tentative Specification USA-LP-91-997A, dated July 7, 1941, the undersigned, Willys-Overland Motors, Inc.

a corporation organized and existing under the laws of the State of Delaware
a partnership consisting of

an individual trading as

of the city of Toledo, O.
hereby proposes to furnish, within the time specified, the materials and supplies at the prices stated opposite the respective items listed on the schedules and agrees upon receipt of written notice of the acceptance of this bid within 10 days (60 days if no shorter period be specified) after the date of opening of the bids, to execute, if required, the Standard Government Form of Contract (Standard Form No. 32) in accordance with the bid as accepted, and to give bond, if required, with good and sufficient surety or sureties, for the faithful performance of the contract, within 10 days after the prescribed forms are presented for signature.

Discount will be allowed for prompt payment as follows: 30 calendar days 1/2 of % percent.

(Time will be computed from date of the delivery of the supplies to carrier when final inspection and acceptance are at point of origin, or from date of delivery at destination or port of embarkation when final inspection and acceptance are at those points, or from date correct bill or voucher properly certified by the contractor is received if the latter date is later than the date of delivery.

(Witness to signature) W. O. Motors, Inc. (Full name of bidder)

By: (Sign in ink)

Title: Chairman of Board

Toledo Ohio (Address)

Continued on 9 sheets, attached hereto, each of which should bear the name of the bidder.

R-79-B

Bantam, Ford and Willys all submitted bids by July 21, 1941, and even the Checker Cab Company submitted a proposal.

Source: United States National Archives, College Park, Maryland

16,000 Awarded to Ford

QM 451 M-P (Proc. 398-42-Neg-1)
Ltr. to the Quartermaster General, 7-30-41, Continued

under their contract, as it has been extended, is now final completion date. The Ford Motor Company on a similar contract for 1500 jobs were scheduled to start delivery March 10th and actually started delivery March 3rd, and although they had a strike at the plant of twenty-three days they completed their contract on May 19, 1941 which was one month ahead of the time scheduled.

8. The real bottleneck in obtaining this type of truck for the Army is in the supplying of axles, transfer cases and universal joints. It will be distinctly an advantage to the Army to have a second source of these units for this type of vehicle of which the Army may eventually require a considerable number. Also the Ford Motor Company, one of the largest producers of motor vehicles in the country, is not being used as a source of supply for any of our tactical vehicles except this 1/4-ton truck. It is the opinion of this office that the additional cost of the Ford vehicles in this particular contract would be of sufficient advantage to the Army in opening up this large source of supply as to warrant the expenditure.

9. Consideration also must be given to the ability to obtain spare parts for the maintenance of these vehicles, and if the contract is awarded to the Ford Motor Company the prompt furnishing of such parts will be more certain and sure than from a smaller company not having the resources that the Ford Motor Company is able to command. Records show that on current orders for spare parts the American Bantam Car Company has been unable to deliver to date any appreciable amount of parts under orders placed May 28, 1941. On the other hand, Ford Motor Company is currently delivering on 90% of the items called for on spare parts orders placed about May 6, 1941.

10. SUMMARY:

a. Ford Motor Company is the only bidder that has made a firm offer as to delivery without qualification.
b. Ford Motor Company is the only bidder who is possessed of the necessary production facilities to perform in accordance with their bid.
c. Ford Motor Company is the only volume motor vehicle manufacturer which is not at present producing vehicles under the Quartermaster Corps motor program.
d. Ford Motor Company is the only bidder which has included in their quotation costs for additional tooling which is required to provide delivery approaching that desired by the War Department, which will also provide duplicate sources for critical component items.
e. Ford Motor Company is the only bidder which, by record of performance, can be expected to deliver service and spare parts concurrently with the vehicles.

257

-3-

23.

The Quartermaster Corps. completed a thorough review of the bids and a technical analysis similar to the process of a year earlier. Their decision on July 30, 1941, "it is therefore recommended...the award for 16,000 1/4-ton trucks be made to the Ford Motor Company..."

Source: United States National Archives, College Park, Maryland

OPM Overrides the Quartermaster

On July 31, 1941, the Quartermaster sought approval from the Secretary of War and Director of Purchases. In yet another stunning reversal, the head of the Office of Production Management, the successor to the National Defense Advisory Commission, William Knudsen overrode the QM's decision.

Source: Public Domain

16,000 Awarded to Willys

WAR DEPARTMENT
OFFICE OF THE QUARTERMASTER GENERAL
WASHINGTON

IN REPLY REFER TO QM 451 M-P
(Neg.-Willys-Overland)

REQUEST FOR CONTRACT CLEARANCE

Date: July 31, 1941.

To: Director of Purchases.

From: The Quartermaster General.

In view of the fact that your office has disapproved our earlier recommendation for the award to Ford Motor Company of 16,000 1/4-ton, 4x4, Trucks in spite of the feeling of this office that the Ford Company was the only bidder qualified to deliver, and in view of the fact that you feel that the Willys-Overland Motors Inc., will deliver in accordance with their bid, because of the urgent need for these vehicles, this office hereby amends the request for clearance attached hereto to request clearance of an award in the usual form as follows:

1. Contractor: Willys-Overland Motors Inc.
   Address: Toledo, Ohio.
   Factory: Toledo, Ohio.
   Delivery: F.o.b. Factory.

2. Description of Material: 16,000 Trucks, 1/4-ton, 4x4, and Parts.

3. Type of Contract: Informal Bid (a).
   Total Price: $13,411,864.40 ($1,432,064.40--Parts).
   Unit Price: $748.74 net.
   Number of Bidders: Four (4)
   Range of Bids: As indicated in the attached copy of Memorandum.

4. Prices last paid and dates: $864.14 net - Contract No. W-398-qm-10263 dated May 24, 1941, with the American Bantam Car Company.

5. Delivery Schedule: Contained in copy of Memorandum attached.

6. The negotiated contract will include an option for increase of award not to exceed fifty percent (50%) of the quantity contracted for, to be exercised within sixty (60) days from and after date of award.

7. No prior approval.

8. No financial aid involved.

9. Attention is invited to the copy of Memorandum inclosed. Execution of negotiated contract with the Willys-Overland Motors Inc., has been approved this date by the Under Secretary of War.

- 1 -

The Quartermaster vigorously objected to Knudsen's decision, but to no avail. Also on July 31, 1941, the Quartermaster sent another approval memo, laced at the top with bitter objections to the decision, but this time awarded the 16,000 to Willys.

Source: United States National Archives, College Park, Maryland

The Willys MB

After the award for the 16,000, the Army continued perfecting the Jeep. Willys named the evolved version the MB—which became the legend of World War II! General George C. Marshall, the Chief of Staff who authorized the Jeep procurement would say that the Jeep represented, "America's greatest contribution to modern warfare." Dwight Eisenhower (pictured) regarded the Jeep as one of the five pieces of equipment most vital to success in Africa and Europe.

Source: Public Domain

Ford to Build Willys Jeeps

EXHIBIT "C"

COPY

Comm. 102

October 10, 1941

FEDERAL TRADE COMMISSION
DOCKET NO. 4959 COMMISSION'S EXHIBIT NO. 102 A
IN THE MATTER OF Willys Overland
DATE 4-19-44 WITNESS Ritter
HOWARD B. SMITH, Official Reporter
By Rosemary Arnold

Contracting Officer
Holabird Quartermaster Depot
Baltimore, Md.

Dear Sir:

We outline below, at your request, a plan by which we can cooperate with you in the establishment of a second entirely independent emergency source for the production of Trucks, 1/4 ton, 4x4, in accordance with our design.

In the event the War Department does standardize upon the vehicle produced by us:

We will, at the request of you or your authorized representative, furnish to any manufacturer designated by you full and complete information necessary to permit such manufacturer to produce vehicles identical with those which are now being produced under Contract No. W398-qm-10757, including Van Dyke drawings, bills of material, material specifications, heat treatment specifications, parts lists, etc., and will at all times keep such information current and furnish complete records of changes made from time to time.

We will furnish the United States, or any manufacturer designated by it, a complete list and details of patents, royalties, patent agreements, license agreements, etc., affecting the manufacture of these vehicles.

We will furnish the United States an irrevocable non-exclusive license to make, have made, to use, maintain and repair, and to sell as surplus or condemned material as provided by law, without payment of royalties, devices embodying the inventions covered by patents owned, controlled or applied for by the Willys-Overland Motors, Inc., which are required in the production of these vehicles. It is, of course, expressly understood that any licenses to use patents owned or controlled by the Willys-Overland Motors, Inc., information, drawings, bills of material, material specifications, heat treatment specifications, parts lists, etc., and records of changes or tools made therefrom, will extend only to the manufacturer of vehicles for the United States Government.

EXHIBIT "A-3" Page 1 Rec. OBTAINED 9/26/42 193 BY N.R. Barrington ATTORNEY EXAMINER

In consideration of the foregoing, it is mutually agreed that:

We will be authorized to complete the building and assembly of, and be awarded contracts for, future requirements of the United States and foreign governments for Trucks, 1/4 ton, 4x4, with due regard for our proven ability to deliver, the delivery requirements of the United States and the maintenance of productive capacity of both sources.

54

The Quartermaster approached Willys in October 1941 with a proposal to have Ford build their MB-vehicle under license. The Toledo manufacturer agreed and they finalized the arrangement by January 1942. Ford would call their version of the vehicle the "GPW" with the W standing for Willys.

Source: Public Domain

Pearl Harbor Attacked

Japan attacked Pearl Harbor, Hawaii on December 7, 1941, thrusting the United States into World War II. War would now test the Jeep like never before.

Source: Public Domain

German Advance is Halted at Moscow's Gates

In December 1941 the Soviet Union halted the German advance at the gates of Moscow. The beleaguered country would fight on.

Source: Public Domain

The MB and GPW in WW II

The MB and GPW served in all theaters of the war in capacities only limited by the imagination. In the photo above, a modified Jeep acts as an ambulance in Australia in the Pacific theater.

Source: Public Domain

EPILOGUE

Bantam's Jeep Legacy

May 20, 1941. Front: Senator Robert Reynolds drives, Senator Claude Pepper holds on. Back: Charles Payne and Harold Crist from Bantam enjoy the ride.

In May 1941, Bantam still had a tailwind pushing them into an imagined triumphant emergence from the Depression. Their work with the U.S. Army lit the fuse that brought into the world a freedom machine. We salute the amazing team that was the American Bantam Car Company.

Source: Claude Pepper Papers, Claude Pepper Library, Florida State University Libraries. Public Domain

Ford's Jeep Legacy

Ford had the size, financing and power that Bantam never had. With seeming ease they stepped up when asked and produced all that the Army wanted from them. In essence, they stood tall as the ultimate team player.

Source: Public Domain

Willys' Jeep Legacy

At the initial bid meeting with the Quartermaster Corps. on July 22, 1940, WIllys looked to have won the day. They lost on a technicality that day after all. Yet they endured several more tightrope reversals and redemptions until they became the big winner in the Jeep derby. Their insistence and persistence upon using their motor look in hindsight like a no-brainer.

Jeep on maneuvers in North Carolina crossing rough terrain pulling a 37-millimeter anti-tank gun. Source: Public Domain

The Jeep's WW II Legacy

Bantam BRC

Willys Quad

Ford Pygmy

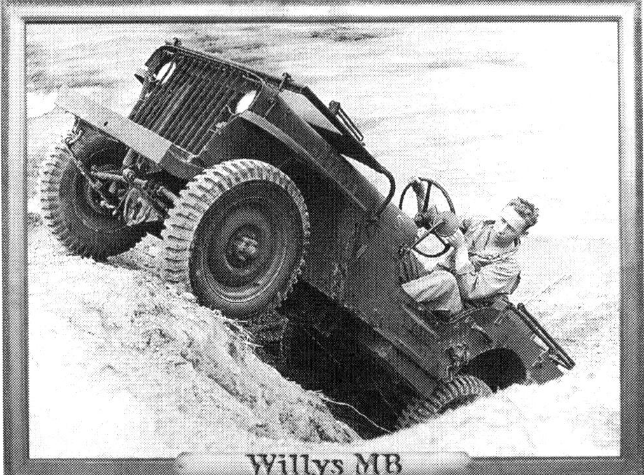
Willys MB

Bantam BRC-40

Willys MA

Ford GP

Bantam would build trailers during the war and limped along until it went out of business in 1956. Willys built 366,000 Jeeps during the war. After the war the company struggled and the Willys name eventually faded into history in 1963. Ford built 277,000 units during the war and remains one of the giants of the automotive industry to this day.

Source: Bantam BRC, upper L, Photo Courtesy of Robert Brandon, Butler, PA. Others: Public Domain

About the Author

Paul Bruno has spent over twenty years researching, writing and studying early Jeep history. He has invested countless hours and treasure to tell this story to the world, first for the big screen and three times in book form. After visiting key sites in the story, and years of research, including at the United States National Archives, he combined his knowledge of project management and history into the 2014 book, *Project Management in History: The First Jeep*. After additional research, he completed *The Original Jeeps* in 2020, which further tells the story of early Jeep history. With a desire to present the events that led to the Jeep for World War II in a unique way he has authored, *The Original Jeeps in Pictures*, which presents the amazing tale in images, thus truly bringing the creation of the Jeep alive as never before. Paul continues his journey into the depths of this important inspirational work of human ingenuity. He has more than 30 years of experience in the fields of project management and information technology. He holds bachelor's degrees in management and computer software as well as a master's degree in business administration and history.

Other Books by the Author:

The Original Jeeps, 2020 ~ *Project Management in History: The First Jeep*, 2014

Articles by the Author:

The Cole-Malley Scandal: Nevada's Political System Revealed: Nevada Historical Society Quarterly, Summer 2007.

Governor James G. Scrugham and Nevada's First Highway Construction Boom: 1923–1927, Nevada Historical Society Quarterly, 2012.

What the World Learned From the Invention of the Jeep: Las Vegas Business Press.

PM History Lessons: *The Jeep*, projectmanagement.com
D-Day, projectmanagement.com
Titanic, projectmanagement.com

About the Publisher

Manuel Freedman, known as Max, has been writing since the 1950's. Currently he writes, produces and coaches screenwriters in the movie industry in Los Angeles, as well as publishes books. The *Original Jeeps in Pictures* is his tenth participation as author, publisher and/or editor in a non-fiction title.

Before starting his media company, Mr. Freedman ran his own advertising and publishing company. There he authored and edited five college-level textbooks for Adobe Systems, which were translated into eight languages and distributed in 35 countries. Three of them are on the subject of computer-based film-making; the other two on publishing. He was born in St. Louis, Missouri, and is a graduate of Stanford University where he was the recipient of a writing scholarship.

Other Books from the Publisher:

The First Jeep by Paul R. Bruno ~ *The Original Jeeps* by Paul R. Bruno
The Great Unconformity by Kate Troll ~ *A'Mused* by Sandy Coccia
Line of Communications by Sondra Garner

Premise of this Volume

The spring and summer of 1940 witnessed the resounding defeat of the French Army and British Expeditionary Force at the hands of a modernized German Army, designed to take advantage of the latest advances in technology. This included mobile vehicles, tanks used in formation to puncture enemy lines, as well as close air support of ground forces. The evacuation of the British from Dunkirk, and the final defeat of their French ally in June 1940, left only a thin line of English fighter planes between that island nation and total defeat.

While events unfolded rapidly in Europe, leaders of the United States Army, decimated by demobilization after World War I and budget cuts during the Great Depression, knew they were completely unprepared for this new type of mobile warfare, called Blitzkrieg or "lightning war." Experts in the Army had worked from the end of World War I to develop a combined light weapons carrier and command/reconnaissance vehicle—but with limited success. In June 1940 the military compiled a list of requirements for a revolutionary new truck to replace the cart and mule as the Army's primary method of moving troops and small payloads.

This book tells the story in images of the American Bantam Car Company, Willys-Overland Motors, Inc., and the Ford Motor Company, who all dared to meet the challenge to build pilot models, and eventually production models, of this vehicle. Their journey throughout 1940 and 1941 comprises a story from which legends come. Overcoming incredible challenges and long odds these firms built the original ¼-ton truck 4x4 "lights", later known as the iconic Jeep.

LOS ANGELES
max@maxfmedia.com

Made in the USA
Columbia, SC
26 January 2023